LEARN Sign Language

in a Hurry

GRASP
THE BASICS OF
American Sign Language
Quickly and Easily

Irene Duke

Avon, Massachusetts

Contains material adapted and abridged from *The Everything® Sign Language
Book, 2nd Edition*, by Irene Duke, copyright © 2009 by F+W Media, Inc.,
ISBN 10: 1-59869-883-4, ISBN 13: 978-1-59869-883-1.

Published by
Adams Media, a division of F+W Media, Inc.
57 Littlefield Street, Avon, MA 02322. U.S.A.
www.adamsmedia.com

ISBN 13: 978-1-4351-4913-7

Printed in the United States of America.

10 9 8 7 6 5 4 3 2

This publication is designed to provide accurate and authoritative information
with regard to the subject matter covered. It is sold with the understanding that
the publisher is not engaged in rendering legal, accounting, or other professional
advice. If legal advice or other expert assistance is required, the services of a
competent professional person should be sought.

—From a *Declaration of Principles* jointly adopted by a Committee of the
American Bar Association and a Committee of Publishers and Associations

Many of the designations used by manufacturers and sellers to distinguish their
product are claimed as trademarks. Where those designations appear in this book
and Adams Media was aware of a trademark claim, the designations have been
printed with initial capital letters.

Interior photographs: Joe Ciarcia / Symphony Photography
Models: Molly Howitt, Tiffany Nardini
Interior illustrations: Elisabeth Lariviere

Contents

Introduction

Whether you're interested in learning sign language because you have a child who is deaf, have lost hearing yourself, need to sign at work, or are simply looking to pick up a new skill, congratulations! You've taken the first step toward learning the art of American Sign Language.

As you'll begin to understand in the upcoming chapters, sign language is more than just a series of hand gestures. It is a natural, flexible way of communicating that will tap your creativity and introduce you to the unique culture of the signing community. Have you ever wondered how babies can learn and communicate with sign language before they can speak? It's because using gestures to communicate with one another is instinctive—it's a natural part of our shared human history. As you'll learn in this book, American Sign Language uses these instinctive hand gestures (such as touching the throat to indicate thirst) coupled with body language and additional signs to incorporate the important elements of expression and intonation into your message.

Learn Sign Language in a Hurry will teach you how to combine natural hand gestures with eye movement, facial expressions, head movement, body posture, and other forms of body language to communicate with and understand people in the Deaf community. After practicing the signs and exercises in this book, you will be able to ask and answer questions, describe an encounter with an old friend, and use signs to paint a visual picture for your audience.

Each chapter in this book will build on the chapter before. You will start out by establishing a basic understanding of the rules of signing, and will then build your vocabulary and confidence as you continue to learn. Like most languages, sign language requires plenty of practice (often in front of a mirror) to get it right, but once you've developed some skill, a whole world of possibility awaits you. And if you need or want to learn basic sign language fast—this is the book for you!

01 / Sign Language Basics

SIGN LANGUAGE IS a complete visual mode of communication. It is the third most used language in the United States and the fourth most used language worldwide. Conversations and information, using sign language, are conveyed visually rather than auditorily and are composed of precise handshapes and movements. Sign language users combine articulate hand movements, facial expressions, and head and body movements to communicate feelings, intentions, humor, complex and abstract ideas, and more.

American Sign Language

American Sign Language, known as ASL, is the natural native language of the American Deaf community. ASL is used as the primary form of communication in the daily lives of the Deaf. ASL is a full language with its own syntax, punctuation, and grammar. American Sign Language is composed of precise handshapes, palm positions, movements, and the use of space around the signer.

These elements, movements, and handshapes, supported by facial expressions and body language, are capable of conveying complex and abstract ideas. ASL is constantly evolving and often changes regionally. The following combined elements serve to make ASL an exciting, effective form of communication:

- ASL signs
- Limited fingerspelling
- Facial expressions
- Body language
- Head movement
- Use of space and directional movement

You will soon acquire, through visual sign images and accompanying instructions, a broad basic sign vocabulary. Please note that all of the images are displayed with the model facing you, the receiver/reader. In other words, simply think that someone is directly signing to you. Also, all images demonstrated throughout this book show a right-handed signer.

Just take a close look at these two images, which illustrate the signs for "hello" and "sign." These two signs are a great beginning and among the most often used signs.

HELLO: The starting position of the hand is similar to a military salute. Then, simply wave your hand off your forehead.

SIGN: Position both hands in front of the chest with both index fingers extended, and palms facing each other. Circle your hands, alternately rotating them toward your body.

Starting Out

The most commonly asked question for beginning signers is "Which hand do I use?" and it is quite easy to answer. You will use your naturally dominant hand. This hand is the one you use daily while writing, eating, and doing most tasks. For those novice signers who are ambidextrous, eventually you will begin to favor one hand, and that will become your dominant hand.

Many signs require the use of both hands, and the use of the dominant hand does not always apply here.

There are three different ways to form signs:

1. **One-handed signs** are formed using only your dominant hand, for example the sign for "mirror."

MIRROR: Form the sign for "mirror" by imitating that you are holding a small vanity mirror and looking into it.

2. **Two-handed symmetrical signs** require the use of both hands moving the same way, formed with the same handshape. Both hands will also be in the same location. See for example the sign for "rain."

RAIN: Form the sign for "rain" with both palms down, fingers spread to an "open five" while dropping your hands down several times to imitate rain.

3. **Two-handed asymmetrical signs** require movement from your dominant active hand while your nondominant hand remains stationary. Often, the nondominant, or motionless, hand acts as a support base for the dominant active hand in these types of signs. For an example see the signs for "sunrise" and "sunset."

Sunrise, Sunset: To sign "sunrise," place your nondominant arm and hand level with your chest. With your dominant hand, form the handshape of a slightly open "C" and bring it upward to a high-noon position; this is "sunrise." Now, bring the arm back down level with the elbow of the nondominant arm, and this represents "sunset."

See the Big Picture

While learning these signs, remember a basic rule of signing: Maintaining eye contact is a must. Breaking eye contact during a signed conversation is considered extremely rude. Learn to develop attentive behaviors during signed conversations, such as nodding and adding an occasional signed exclamation, like "Yes," "Wow," or "Really," just as you would in an oral conversation. In addition, observing the signer's face at all times assists comprehension. Do not worry about focusing on the hands of the signer. Learn to see the whole picture, face and hands simultaneously.

The Big Four: Rules of Use

It is important to know the rules governing the proper use of sign language. The explanation of the rules called the "Big Four" will add clarity to the important elements in sign language.

A sign is a unit of language that is formed with distinctive handshapes, locations, specific movements, and facial expressions. The signs have four independent parts. These parts play exacting roles, and if any one of them is changed, the meaning of the sign is altered. Take a close look at these four important parts of signs:

1. Handshape
2. Location
3. Movement
4. Palm position

Handshape

The term *handshape* refers to the specific shape of your hand while you are forming the sign. The handshapes could be the letters of the alphabet or numbers. Most importantly, most handshapes have specific names: "claw hand," "open five," "flat hand," and so forth. The names of the handshapes are an important element to memorize. As a novice signer, memorizing the handshape names will be a very important tool. The reason is quite simple; this book, all sign language dictionaries, and ASL instructors use the names of handshapes when giving instruction on how to form a sign. Changing the handshape of a sign will change the meaning of a sign.

The following images are a selection of the most commonly used handshapes and their names:

One Hand: Hold your index finger upright in the vertical position, palm forward, all other fingers tucked away.

Claw Hand: Bend all your fingers and thumb slightly separated, imitating the shape of a claw.

Curved Hand: Make the handshape of "C" and tuck your thumb against the side of your hand.

Flat Hand: Extend all your fingers with your thumb neatly tucked against the side of your hand.

Open Five: Spread apart all your fingers and your thumb.

Bent Hand: Bend your hand at the large knuckles and tuck your thumb against the side of your hand.

MODIFIED "O/AND" HAND: Close your hand so all fingers and thumb are touching. Often, this handshape is referred to as the "and" hand.

Location

The term *location* describes where you place and form the sign. Location is an important factor because if you change it, you will change the meaning of the sign. The signs for "mother" and "father" are a good example of this concept. The signs for "mother" and "father" have the same handshape, an open five. However, the meaning is changed when that same handshape is placed in different locations. The location of these two signs indicates the genders.

MOTHER: Tap the thumb of the "open five" hand on the chin.

FATHER: Tap the thumb of the "open five" hand on the forehead.

The consistency of the principles of ASL makes your learning curve easier. All female signs will be formed in the jaw line area, though the handshape might be a little different for sister, aunt, or female cousin. All male signs will be formed in the area of the forehead; although the handshape for brother, uncle, or male cousin may be different, the location does not change.

MALE: Move the "modified O" hand slightly away from the forehead. All male signs are made in the area of the forehead. Hint: Imitate tipping the brim of a hat.

FEMALE: Stroke the extended thumb of the "A" hand down, along the jaw line. All female signs are made in the area of the jaw line. Hint: Think of tying a bonnet.

Movement

The term *movement* describes the action that makes the sign, such as moving in a circle, up and down, forward or backward. An example would be using the index finger and pointing upward. This movement forms the sign "up." Using the index finger and pointing downward forms the sign "down." There are many signs just like the ones described, such as "in/out" and "come/go." Simply changing the movement changes the meaning of the sign.

Often, the novice signer incorrectly uses the signs "in" and "out" while signing sentences. Here are a few examples to help you:

■ **In:** The correct application for this form of "in" would be if you are putting a pencil "in" a box or putting contacts "in" your cell phone or e-mail.

The incorrect usage of this sign for "in" would be if it was applied while signing, "in spring." The correct sign would be "during" spring.

■ **Out:** The correct application for this form of "out" would be when signing "take the roast 'out' of the oven." The incorrect usage of this "out" would be if it was formed while signing, "go out to play."

IN/OUT: To sign "in," put the right modified "O" hand into the left "C" hand; to sign "out," pull the right modified "O" hand out of the left "C" hand.

Palm Position

The term *palm position* refers to the position of the palms of your hands and the direction the palm is facing. For example, placing your palm on your own chest would mean "my/mine." Facing your palm toward the reader would translate to "your."

MINE: Place your "flat" hand, palm inward on your chest.

YOUR: Move your "flat" hand, palm forward, toward the reader.

You should take a quick look at the following definitions and explanations of the palm positions. You will see these descriptive terms used in this book, ASL dictionaries, and instructional texts.

- "Forward"—Palms are facing away from the body
- "Inward"—Palms are facing toward the body
- "Horizontal"—Palms are parallel to the floor
- "Palm toward palm"—Palms are facing each other
- "Palm-to-palm"—Palms are applied to each other

Intonation and Sign Order

Intonation in sign language is created in a variety of ways. A sign can be formed with intensity to show intonation. For instance, if you worked hard all day, you might form the sign "work" by striking the "S" hands together with noticeable force.

Another way to show intonation is to execute a sign with varying degrees of speed. If you were signing you had to go somewhere in a hurry, you would sign that with a quick snapping motion. On the other hand, if you were just taking a nice slow drive, you would sign that slowly, with the appropriate casual facial expression. Another way of expressing intonation is by using facial expression along with intensity and motion.

When you want to express that you love something you would sign "love" by gently crossing your arms over your chest. However, if you are madly in love with something or someone, then you would make the same sign tightly, hugging your chest and perhaps rocking back and forth and adding a big delightful smile. These movements, along with your facial expression, instantly add a strong degree to the word "love." See the following page for an example.

Like intonation, ASL syntax—that is, sign order—is often difficult to master during the early part of the process of acquiring signing skills. The syntax when signing generally follows this order: object, subject, verb. Time, if applicable, is signed at the beginning of the sentence and often signed again at the end of the sentence. However, ASL syntax is often varied in short sentences. It also varies regionally. For instance, the order could be seen as subject, verb, and object. This is made with modifications, including omitting any "to be" verbs.

Love: Cross both arms and hug your chest. This sign can be formed with either closed fists or open palms.

Plurals

There are many different ways to pluralize signs in ASL. The easiest way to pluralize a sign, for a novice signer, is to simply re-sign it two or more times. For instance, the sign for tree, when reduplicated, becomes forest. The sign for child, when made multiple times, becomes children. The following are ways to pluralize signs:

- Form the sign, repeat the sign to pluralize two, three, or more of the same item.
- A sweep: A signer can use the index finger and sweep out and in front of the body to indicate a multiple number, such as "they" or "them," or a flock.
- Numbers: Sign the object or thing and add the numbers. (Chapter 5)
- Quantifiers: Sign the object or thing and add signs such as "many" or "little."
- Classifiers: Sign the object or thing incorporating classifiers, which demonstrate shape, group, quantity, and movement. (Chapter 3)

First Signs: The Manual Alphabet

Before you begin forming the letters of the manual alphabet, you'll need to get into the proper position and learn special strategies to become a good fingerspeller. The following are some tips to ensure accurate fingerspelling:

- Make sure your palm faces the receiver/reader.
- Make sure your elbow is close to your body.

- Hold your dominant hand slightly to the right of your face and just below the chin.
- Do not bounce the letters.
- Speed is not important; it is the clarity of the formation of each letter that matters.
- Do not say or mouth single letters.

Now you are ready to form the handshapes of the letters of the manual alphabet. Remember, you will be looking at the back of your hand, so try practicing in a mirror.

"A" Hand: Make a fist with your dominant hand. Make sure your thumb is on the side of the fist and not within it.

"B" Hand: All fingers are vertical and pressed together and your thumb is curled in to your palm.

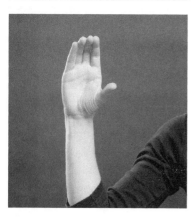

"C" Hand: Form a "C" with all fingers neatly together. Your palm is facing left.

"D" Hand: Curl all your fingers down onto thumb except for the index finger, which remains vertical. Hint: "Dump" all your fingers on the thumb except the index finger. So remember, the next time you are practicing the letter "D," say the word "dump" for a clue.

"E" Hand: Curl all fingers down and tuck the thumb into the palm.

"F" Hand: Pinch the index finger to the thumb. Middle, ring, and pinky fingers are vertical. Hint: Imagine the last three fingers as a mini flag.

"G" Hand: Extend your thumb and index finger facing left, position hand facing slightly left. Middle, ring, and pinky fingers are tucked into palm.

"H" Hand: Place your index finger on top of your middle finger facing left, with your thumb tucked away behind the two fingers.

"I" Hand: Make a fist, hold your pinky finger vertical.

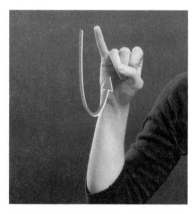

"J" Hand: Make a fist, hold your pinky finger vertical, and draw a "J" shape inward. Hint: "J" is the same handshape as "I" with a simple movement added.

"K" Hand: Place your thumb between your index and middle fingers, which are held vertically. Ring and pinky fingers are tucked into the palm.

"L" Hand: Make a fist, leave your index finger vertical and extend the thumb.

"M" Hand: Tuck your thumb into palm, then wrap your index, middle, and ring fingers over the thumb. Hint: Visualize a lowercase "m" with its three lines, thus the three fingers.

"N" Hand: Tuck your thumb into palm, then wrap your index and middle fingers over the thumb. Hint: Visualize a lowercase "n" with its two lines, thus the two fingers.

"O" Hand: Form a nice round "O" by resting all the fingers on the thumb.

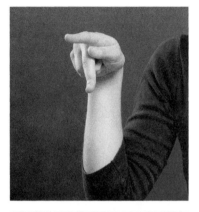

"P" Hand: Place your thumb between the index and middle fingers. Ring and pinky fingers are tucked into the palm. Drop your wrist downward. Hint: The letter "P" is made the same as the letter "K," except, the P "points" downward.

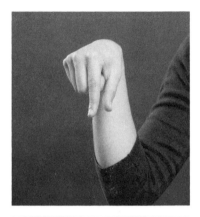

"Q" Hand: Extend your thumb and index finger downward. Tuck middle, ring, and pinky fingers into your palm. Hint: The letter "Q" is made like the letter "G," but with the wrist downward.

"R" Hand: Cross your index and middle fingers. Thumb, ring, and pinky fingers are tucked into palm.

"S" Hand: Make a fist, place your thumb in front of your fingers. Hint: The letters "A" and "S" are easily confused. For "A," place your thumb on the side of your fist: for "S," place and "show" your thumb in front of your fingers.

"T" Hand: Make a fist. Tuck your thumb between your index and middle fingers.

"U" Hand: Hold your index and middle fingers vertical. Tuck your thumb, ring, and pinky fingers into your palm.

"V" Hand: Your index and middle fingers are held vertical and spread open, creating a "V." Tuck your thumb, ring, and pinky fingers into your palm.

"W" Hand: Your index, middle, and ring fingers are held vertical and spread open, creating a "W." Hold your pinky finger down with your thumb.

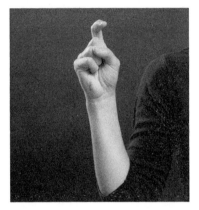

"X" Hand: Make a fist leaving your index finger vertical but bent into a hook shape.

"Y" Hand: Extend your thumb and pinky finger. Tuck your index, middle, and ring fingers into your palm.

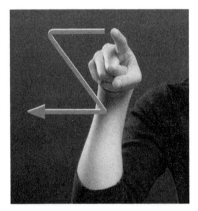

"Z" Hand: Make a fist with your index finger extended, then make the shape of the letter "Z" in the air.

Using this chart, practice forming the letters by groups:

- A, E, O, M, N, S, and T are formed with a closed hand.
- B, C, D, F, I, K, L, R, U, V, W, X, and Y are formed in a vertical position.
- G and H are formed in a horizontal position.
- P and Q are formed in a downward position.
- J and Z are formed with added movement of tracing the letter.

"I Love You" is one of the most popular acronym signs and is easily recognized. The characteristics of this handshape are what bring forth the meaning. The vertical pinky represents the letter "I." The index finger and extended thumb represent the "L" in "love." The combination of the pinky and the thumb extended represent the letter "Y" for "you."

I Love You: Combining the letters "I," "L," and "Y" on one hand forms the "I Love You" sign.

Fingerspelling

Fingerspelling is using the letter representations of the twenty-six letters of the alphabet to spell out words. The use of fingerspelling is limited in ASL. It is primarily used to communicate places and names when no formal recognized signs exist.

When you don't know a sign for a word, first try to describe it by acting it out, pointing, miming, or drawing it. In other words, don't use fingerspelling as your first choice when you don't know a sign. Fingerspelling is not a substitute for signing; it is used for words when a sign does not exist. In ASL, fingerspelling should only be used for the following situations:

- Proper names
- Names of towns, cities, and states
- Specific brand names of products or services
- Titles of books and movies

Now that you know the manual alphabet, it's time to practice fingerspelling three-letter words. A great way to practice is to use a spelling bee game. The movement from letter to letter will improve the agility of your fingers. Later, you and a fingerspelling partner can practice the spelling bee game together. Haven't found a partner yet? Well, do your best to locate one, and remember: To teach is to relearn.

The instructions for the spelling bee with a partner are as follows. Working from a list, each person alternately and randomly selects a word to fingerspell. The receiver must correctly fingerspell the word back to the sender. Each word is then checked off. Continue in this fashion until you have fingerspelled all the words. Try making the game a little more difficult. Create a new list of fifty words. This time, these words should be four to five letters in length. You can continue playing the spelling bee game in this same fashion by simply increasing the length and difficulty of the words.

cat	mop	top	tap	nap
tip	bag	pit	hat	lip
mug	hit	sip	zip	lug
dim	pie	eye	hug	dye
sag	zap	cap	bit	but
wax	oar	not	get	fit
eat	jar	box	rat	six
van	gin	gym	sir	was
oat	fox	ear	jam	kit
raw	get	jaw	wet	nip

Initialized Signs

Initialized signs, also known as borrowed signs, are signs that—in general—borrow the first letter of words. Below is a list of "initialized" signs. These signed words require placing and/or moving a letter of the manual alphabet in specific locations on or around the body. When you are finished signing this list, you will know twenty-six new initialized signs!

The Sign	*The Letter*
Attitude	Tap the "A" hand on the heart.
Boss	Tap the "B" hand on the heart.
Coach	Tap the "C" hand on the top of the right shoulder.
Dentist	Stroke the "D" hand back and forth in front of the teeth.
Elevator	Raise the "E" hand up and down in front of the body.
Feather	Slide the "F" hand over the top of the ear.
Glasses	Stroke the "G" hand along the frame of an imaginary pair of glasses.
Hospital	Use the "H" hand to form a cross on the upper left arm.
Idea	Place the "I" hand on the temple and move forward slightly.
Jeans	Use the "J" hand and trace a "J" movement near the waist/hip area.
King	Tap the "K" hand on the left shoulder, then down on the right hip.
Loser	Place the "L" hand in the middle of the forehead.
Medical	Tap the "M" hand on the inside of the left wrist.
Nurse	Tap the "N" hand on the inside of the left wrist.
Opinion	Place the "O" hand on the temple and move forward slightly.
Prince	Tap the "P" hand on the left shoulder, then down on the right hip.
Queen	Tap the "Q" hand on the left shoulder, then down on the right hip.
Rose	Tap the "R" hand under each nostril.
South	Move the "S" hand straight down.
Toilet	Shake the "T" hand.
Uncle	Hold the "U" hand near the temple and slightly shake back and forth from the wrist.
Vegetable	Tap the "V" hand on each corner of the mouth.
Water	Tap the "W" hand just below the lower lip.
Xylophone	Tap both "X" hands alternately, imitating playing the xylophone.
Yellow	Shake the "Y" hand.
Zoo	Form the letters "Z," "O," and "O," while moving slightly to the right.

Fingerspelled Loan Signs

Another way the letters of the manual alphabet are used is in the application of fingerspelled "loan signs" and fingerspelled abbreviations. "Loan signs" have unique patterns and movements. They normally have two to five letters, and they are commonly used words. These words are all formed and shaped in various patterns, like so:

- "Bus" is fingerspelled using the letters "B" to "S" in a vertical, downward movement.
- "All" is fingerspelled using the letters "A" to "L" in a sweeping movement from left to right.
- "Dog" is fingerspelled using the letters "D" to "G" as if snapping the fingers.
- "Apt" is fingerspelled using the letters "A," "P," and "T," with a quick down and up flick of the wrist.
- "Refrigerator" is fingerspelled using the letters "R," "E," and "F" in a vertical downward motion.

The loan signs that you have just signed have been developed over a period of time and have proven to be an expedient way of signing these words. These loan signs, through time and by their appearance and movement, have become accepted signs in their loan format. However, for the novice signer, keep in mind the above words also have regular whole ASL signs.

02 / Understanding, Asking, and Answering Questions

IN DAILY CONVERSATION, you ask and answer questions constantly; questions are a basic and extremely useful part of both spoken and visual languages, and are especially important when you are learning to sign. In order to communicate effectively using ASL, you'll need to learn how to ask and answer questions, including one especially important one: "What time is it?"

"Wh" Questions and "Yes-No" Questions

The strong visual aspects of sign language require that questions be divided into two categories. The first category is the "wh-" words: who, what, when, where, why, which, and how. Questions that use these words ask for specific information. The second category is "yes-no" questions. These questions can be answered with a simple yes or no.

Both of these question types need to be supported by specific facial expressions with nonmanual behaviors. Nonmanual behaviors do not use the hands. Instead, these behaviors use the eyes, facial expressions, head movement, body posture, or body language. Signers use nonmanual behaviors to show emotion, emphasize a point, make a negative statement, and ask questions. Facial expressions are equal to vocal intonation. When you do not apply the proper facial expressions and nonmanual behaviors, your questions may not be interpreted correctly.

Trying Out Nonmanual Behaviors

As a novice signer, your first step toward acquiring the important elements of facial expressions and nonmanual behaviors begins right here, with the two categories of questions. The skill of applying facial expression and nonmanual behaviors will gradually build and develop naturally as you further your studies in sign language.

Wh- Word Questions

When asking a wh- word question, do the following:

- Furrow your eyebrows
- Tilt your head forward
- Make direct eye contact
- Hold your last sign

Yes-No Questions

When asking a yes-no question, do the following:

- Raise your eyebrows to widen your eyes
- Tilt your head slightly forward
- Make direct eye contact
- Hold the last sign in your sentence

Occasionally, a yes-no question is also accompanied by a question mark.

Question mark: Use your index finger and trace a question mark exactly as you would write it.

Signing Wh- Words

Now it's time to sign the wh- words with the appropriate facial expressions.

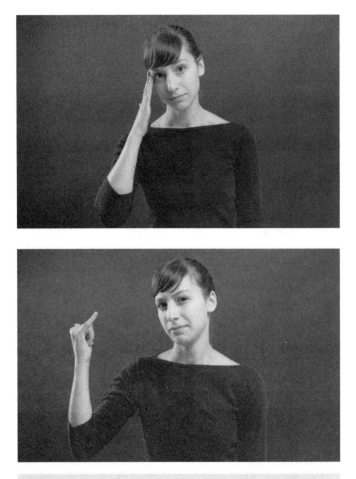

WHY (above): Place the fingertips on your temple and pull down and out, forming into the letter "Y." *Variation (below):* This variation is commonly used; place the fingertips on the temple and pull down and out while wiggling the bent middle finger.

Answering Questions

It's not enough to just be able to ask questions. You'll also need to know how to answer them, of course. In just a moment, you will go through an exercise in which you will sign both the questions and the answers. You will be using signs you just learned, "my/mine" and "your," in the exercise. In addition, you need to add a few more signs to your growing vocabulary list.

YES: Shake the "S" hand up and down. An affirmative head nod should always accompany this sign.

NO: Touch your index and middle fingers quickly to your extended thumb. The sign for "no" is small and can be easily missed. A negative headshake should always accompany this sign as it ensures your answer.

NAME: Cross and tap the "H" hands twice.

I, ME: Use your index finger and point to the center of your chest.

LIVE/ADDRESS: Use both "A" hands, palms facing your body, starting at the lower chest and moving upward. *Variation:* Use both "L" hands, palms facing the body, starting at the lower chest and moving upward.

HOUSE: Touch the fingertips of the "flat" hands, palms facing and forming a peak, imitating the roof of a house.

CITY, TOWN, COMMUNITY: Touch the fingertips of the "flat" hands, palms facing and forming a "peak," tap, and slightly twist several times, imitating multiple roofs. *Variation:* Touch the fingertips of the "flat" hands, palms facing and forming a "peak," tap and separate two or three times while moving the house/ buildings to the side.

WORK: Use both "S "hands, palms facing down, tap your right wrist on the back of your left fist a few times.

LEARN: Place all the fingertips of your right hand into your left palm. Next pull up your right hand with a modified "O" and place it on your forehead. *Note*: The action of the sign suggests putting knowledge into the mind.

DEAF: Use your index finger and touch your cheek near the ear, and then near the corner of your mouth.

MEET: Hold your right and left index fingers upward, palms facing, then bring the hands together until they meet.

NICE: Use right and left "flat" hands, slide the palm of your right hand forward across the left upturned palm, imitating cleaning a counter.

To sign "nice to meet you," combine "nice" and "meet" only. There is no need to sign "you"; this information is provided by the directionality of the sign "meet." See previous page for an example.

The signs for "excuse" and "nice" closely resemble each other and are often confused. "Excuse" is signed with a "curved" hand. "Nice" is signed with a "flat" hand and is also used to sign the word "clean."

Practice Interview

Looking at the following interview, you will notice that the questions are written in English order and then the questions are written in approximate ASL sign order. The answers are presented in a simple ASL sign order. At first, this sign order will sound strange to your auditory ear. You must keep in mind that sign language is a *visual* language. Therefore, how it sounds grammatically is not relative to the way it is received through the eyes. The sign order, as written, is perfectly acceptable.

▶ **The Interview Questions**

English	*ASL*	*Response*
What is your name?	Name your?	Name my (fingerspell name)
What city do you live in?	City where live?	Live/address (fingerspell town)
Where do you work?	Work where?	Work (fingerspell workplace)
Where are you learning ASL?	ASL learn where?	ASL learn (fingerspell college)
Are you deaf?	Deaf (sign a question mark)	Yes/No
Nice to meet you.	Nice meet.	Nice-meet-you.

You have just learned how to sign everyday questions and responses! Don't let the ASL order and sound of these sentences concern you. Signing "name my" without the word "is" is perfectly acceptable. Adapting to ASL sign order, facial expressions, and nonmanual behaviors are skills that develop slowly with practice and experience. At this point, your primary focus is learning to form the signs accurately, while gradually learning how to apply these additional elements.

It is important to begin to develop a comfort level. In a conversation with a member of the Deaf community, that person may ask many questions to establish a connection between you and the Deaf community. In doing so, you may be asked these additional questions:

■ Do you have a deaf family member?
■ Why are you learning sign language?
■ Who is your teacher?

Regardless of whether you ever have the experience of meeting a member of the Deaf community, you will still need these common, everyday question signs.

Explaining Relationships
As you begin to answer questions in more detail, you will want to talk about some of the important people in your life. In this section you'll learn the signs for all of these special people, continuing to build your signing vocabulary.

Assigning Gender
Gender is easy to specify: All female signs are formed by stroking the jaw line. All male signs are signed from the forehead. Here are two excellent memory aids:

■ Male: Visualize tipping the brim of a baseball hat.
■ Female: Visualize tying the strings of a bonnet.

The next set of signs involves gender. Before beginning, it is worth revisiting Chapter 1 to look again at the images for "male" and "female."

Family Relationships
Next, you'll learn how to be more specific with gender signs. In general, you will learn to sign gender first followed by a second sign that is appropriate to the meaning or the clarification. Once again, a series of two or more signs is called a compound sign. Let's begin with the sign for "family," which demonstrates unity.

FAMILY: Hold the "F" hands close to your body, thumb tips touching, move both hands out in a circular movement until both sides of your pinky fingers touch.

Now that you know how to sign "family," using the same form you can also sign "team" using the letter "T," "class" using the letter "C," and "group" using the letter "G."

CHILD: The sign for "child" can indicate various ages. Just extend your arm, and raise it to the age-appropriate height.

If you want to sign "children," all you need to do is pat the heads of several imaginary "children" all around you.

Signing "baby" or "infant" is easy. It is a natural gesture. You need only to imitate holding and rocking a baby in your arms.

The signs for father and mother were introduced in Chapter 1. Now, here are common variations to these two signs:

- Variation on father: To sign "father," place the thumb of your "open five" hand on your forehead and wiggle your fingers.

- Variation on mother: Place the thumb of your "open five" hand on your jawline and wiggle your fingers.

Signing "grandfather" and "grandmother" is quite easy. You will only need to add a forward movement.

- **To sign grandfather**: First sign "father," then move forward with a large arched movement off your forehead. This movement indicates generations.

  Variation: First sign "father," then move forward with two small arcs off your jaw or chin.

- **To sign grandmother**: First sign "mother," then move forward with a large arched movement off your forehead.

  Variation: First sign "mother," then move forward with two small arcs off your jaw or chin.

MARRIAGE: To sign "marriage," tightly seal both hands together, representing a bond.

Now that you have learned how to sign "marriage," you are able to form the compound sign for "husband" and "wife." To form these signs, you will need to sign the gender first, then the sign for "marriage." In other words, sign "female" and "marriage" for "wife." Sign "male" and "marriage" for "husband."

The signs for "brother" and "sister" are also compound signs. This image demonstrates the faster and more popular variation.

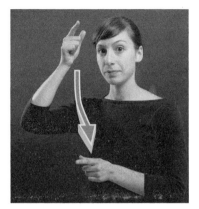

BROTHER: Tap the slightly extended thumb tip of the right "G" hand on your forehead, bring your right hand down, and place it on the left "G" hand in front of your body.

SISTER: Tap the slightly extended thumb tip of the right "G" hand on your jawline, bring your right hand down, and place it on the left "G" hand in front of your body.

By this time, you should have mastered the location of the female and male signs. Having mastered genders, you can easily sign the remaining family members. These signs are initialized in their appropriate gender locations:

- **Uncle**: Hold the "U" hand near your temple and shake slightly back and forth from your wrist.
- **Nephew**: Extend the fingers of the "N" hand toward your temple and shake slightly back and forth from your wrist.
- **Niece**: Extend the fingers of the "N" hand toward your jaw line and shake slightly back and forth from your wrist.
- **Aunt**: Hold the "A" hand near your jaw line and shake slightly back and forth from your wrist.

People You Know

In this section, you will learn to affix the "person" sign to create compound signs used to describe people. (Of course, the "person" sign can also be used alone to simply mean "person.") Learning to affix or apply the "person" sign gives you a powerful tool for communication. When the "person" sign is used as an ending, it can be referred to in sign language dictionaries as any of the following: "person," "agent," or the "er" sign. This book will refer to it as the "person" sign.

When the "person" sign is applied to a sign, it is now considered a compound sign and adds clarity. This compound sign identifies whether you are talking about an item or a person. For example, you can imitate playing the piano, and this is clearly understood when signed. However, if you want to sign "pianist," you imitate playing a "piano" then add the "person" sign. Another example is to sign "write" then add the "person" sign to signify that you mean "writer" or "author." With one sign, you can also change a sport into the "player" of that sport.

Two for One

In this section, you will learn to sign vocabulary words simultaneously. First, you will learn to sign a noun or verb. Next, you will sign that noun or verb followed by the "person" sign. The signs for interpreter, teacher, and lawyer require adding the "person" sign.

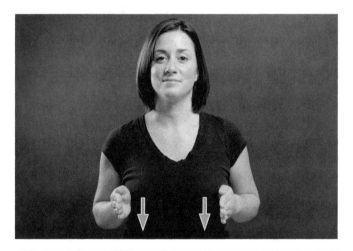

PERSON: Use both "flat" hands, palms facing each other, and move hands straight down in front of your body.

Look at each of the following images and learn how to sign them.

INTERPRET: Twist the "F" hands alternately back and forth. To sign "interpreter," twist the "F" hands alternately back and forth, and add the "person" sign. *Memory aid*: The movement of the hands depicts translating back and forth between people.

TEACH: Move both modified "O" hands forward from your forehead. To sign "teacher," move both modified "O" hands forward from your forehead, and add the "person" sign. *Memory aid*: The hands moving forward from your forehead represent taking knowledge from the mind and giving it forth to the learners.

LAW: Slide the right "L" hand in the left vertical hand from the fingertips to your wrist. To sign "lawyer," slide the right "L" hand in the left vertical hand from the fingertips to your wrist, and add the "person" sign. *Memory aid*: The "L" in the hand represents the book of *Laws and Rules*.

Not all signs affix or use the "person" sign to refer to occupations or sports. Here you will also learn a few signs that do not require affixing the "person" sign.

The signs for "dentist" are representative of how nicely signs evolve with the change in times. Hitting your jaw line with the "S" hand was an early sign. This sign represented silver being hammered into teeth for fillings or a very bad toothache. This version is used for a bad toothache. Next, the generic version is tapping a tooth with the index finger then adding the "person" sign. Another version is the initialized sign, which has you tap your teeth with the "D" hand. Today, there is a brighter smiling variation of "dentist." This sign reflects the new attitude of painless dentistry and the bright white smile of healthy teeth.

DENTIST: Smile while moving the "D" hand slightly back and forth in forth in front of your teeth.

Pronouns and Possessives

If you have the opportunity to go to a social event in the Deaf community, you will see a room come alive with signs, natural gestures, facial expressions, and body language. The Deaf are fabulous storytellers and easily capture your attention with the full animation that rounds out their storytelling. Building on what you've just learned about asking and answering questions and describing your relationships, let's learn possessives and a few pronouns to continue building your ASL skills. Possessives and pronouns will help you better express yourself and provide a greater level of detail for the person you are having a signed conversation with.

YOU: Point the index finger of the "one" hand toward the person.

In sign language, pointing is referred to as "indexing." This is an appropriate and important element in this visual language.

To sign "they," "them," "these," and "those," use the same sign form as "you," adding a sweeping movement in the direction of the objects or subjects.

US, WE: Use the handshape of "K," palm facing your right shoulder, and extend your arm back and forth. The sign for "we" and "us" uses a form of indexing. Instead of pointing to the person and then to yourself, this sign simply swings back and forth between you and an imaginary or real person. *Variation:* To sign "we," tap the index finger of the "one" hand on the right shoulder then sweep across the chest and tap the left shoulder.

Possessives

In Chapter 1, you learned how to form two possessive signs, "my/mine" and "your." This section will extend the application and uses for the sign "your." If you have forgotten how to form this sign, return to the chapter and take a quick look at the image. To begin, sign "your," which is the basic root sign for yours, theirs, his, and hers. To sign all of these words, all you need to do is make a few directional changes and/or add a sign.

■ To sign "your," use the "flat" hand, palm facing forward, extend the arm forward toward the person. This sign is the root for the following signs.

■ To sign "yours," and "theirs," use the "flat" hand for "your," palm facing forward, now move your hand with an extended arm left to right across the front of your body.

Should you have a need to be gender specific, you are now ready to learn how to sign "his" and "hers." The signs for "his" and "hers" are compound signs. A compound sign uses two or more signs to convey an idea.

■ To indicate "his," sign "male" first, followed by the sign for "your."

■ To indicate "hers," sign "female" first, followed by the sign for "your."

THING, THINGS: Move the "flat" hand, palm up, forward and slightly to the right.

If you have lots of things, what-cha-ma-call-its, or thing-a-ma-bobs, simply swing out your right hand and then your left hand. You can also add small up-and-down bobble movements when moving this sign, demonstrating "lots of stuff." The possessive signs you have just learned are important and used frequently in our daily conversations.

03 / Adding Color to Your Vocabulary

CONVERSATION IS FULL of description; it's what adds fun to the otherwise mundane. In this chapter, you will learn how to use descriptions to identify someone and to express your emotions and feelings. In addition, there will be a few dashes of color thrown in just to make it even more exciting.

Describing People

People are very different from one another. Think of how boring the world would be if everyone were the same! Things like hair color, height, and eye color are all characteristics that distinguish an individual. People use these characteristics to describe others. In sign language, there are certain rules to follow for describing people.

Descriptions of people tend to follow a particular order, and gender is always mentioned first. It is followed by the height, color of the hair and hairstyle, and body type. If the person being described has any distinguishing features, these can then also be described. For example, someone may have a very large smile, beautiful green eyes, or perhaps a certain mannerism.

The sign for "face" is formed by circling your face with the index finger. Touching or stroking your hair forms the sign for "hair." When you want to describe someone's hairstyle, you simply mime the hairstyle. Perhaps you have used mime when describing someone with a mustache or beard. Natural gestures serve as wonderful enhancers to signing. It is perfectly okay to use them. In fact, you are encouraged to use natural gestures, facial expressions, and body language.

Playing with Color

Learning to sign colors in groups according to location (that is, where on the body they are signed) is the best way to put them to memory. All the colors that are signed on the face are described here and some are illustrated with images.

- Pink and red are formed on the lips.
- Brown and tan are stroked on the side of the face.
- Orange is squeezed on the cheek.
- Black is formed on the eyebrow.

COLORS: Wiggle your four fingers slightly at the mouth.

PINK: Stroke your middle finger tip of the "P" hand near your lower lip.

RED: Stroke your index finger down your lips. *Variation:* Red can also be signed using the letter "R" stroked down the lips. This version is an "initialized" sign.

BROWN: Draw the "B" hand down your cheek.

ORANGE: Squeeze the "S" hand in the cheek area.

BLACK: Draw your slightly hooked index finger across the eyebrow.

The next set of colors is signed using initializing. These colors are formed in the fingerspelling space with the added element of gently "shaking" the letters.

BLUE: Shake the "B" hand gently side to side.

GREEN: Shake the "G" hand gently side to side.

PURPLE: Shake the "P" hand gently side to side.

YELLOW: Shake the "Y" hand gently side to side.

WHITE: Draw the "open five" hand forward from your chest. Close hand to a modified "O."

The sign for "gray" is a good demonstration of out with the old, and in with the new. The oldest version of "gray" was a combination of three signs. That version was shortened and what was left was a sign best used to describe the concept of gray versus the color. Today's version of "gray" stays in the same sign form as the other colors that are signed in the fingerspelling space, such as yellow and purple. Signing the new way for "gray" is unique. A combination of the two letters "G" and "R" are formed on one hand.

GRAY: Form the letter "G," then cross your index and middle fingers to form the letter "R," creating a combination of the letters "G" and "R." Shake gently back and forth.

Getting Dressed

Your visualization and mime skills will be put to the test in this section as you learn how to describe apparel. First, start with the easy stuff. To sign "shirt," all you need to do is tug on your shirt. See how simple that is? You can describe the sleeve lengths of shirts with visualization. Just extend your left arm and tap at the appropriate length with the side of the "B" hand: Tap the wrist for long sleeves, the forearm for three-quarter-length sleeves, and the upper arm for short sleeves. Generally, you can point to any item of clothing in order to describe it.

Still stimulating your visualization and mime skills, let's picture putting on a pair of pants. In order for you to put them on, you need to pull them up. Okay, so guess how you sign pants. If you answered pulling them up to the waist, you are correct! Of course, an outfit wouldn't be complete without a pair of shoes.

SHOES: Tap the "S" hands together twice. *Memory aid:* Visualize Dorothy in *The Wizard of Oz* clicking the heels of her shiny ruby red shoes.

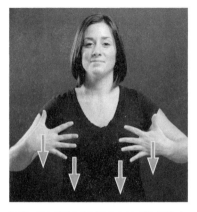

CLOTHES: Sweep both "open five" hands down over the front of your body once or twice.

SHIRT, BLOUSE: Use the index finger and thumb of both hands, just below your shoulders, to pinch the fabric and tug forward twice. *Variation:* To sign "blouse," use both index fingers, tap your shoulders, and tap at the waist.

Be careful when using one hand for the sign for shirt; one hand means "volunteer." However, if the subject of the conversation is "clothing," then using one hand to sign "shirt" is acceptable.

Today's style of clothing favors the T-shirt for comfort and leisure wear. Forming the sign for T-shirt is quick and easy just by using the letter "T" from the alphabet. To sign "T-shirt," stroke the letter "T" downward on the front of your chest.

PANTS: Place both "open" hands at the waist, and imitate pulling on a pair of pants.

To sign "shorts," first make the sign for pants then use the edge of both "flat" hands palms up to draw the desired length across the thighs or knees.

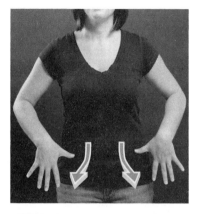

SKIRT: Sweep both "open five" hands down from your waist and out to the sides a few times.

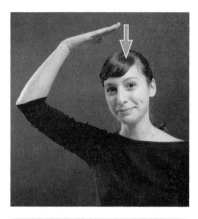

HAT: Tap the top of your head with a "flat " hand.

COAT: Hold the "A" hands in front of your shoulders and imitate putting on a coat with a sweeping downward movement.

Describing the "Look"

They say that beauty is in the eye of the beholder. The sign for "beautiful" can be communicated with added emphasis by using your eyes and facial expressions. This is especially true if you are trying to describe someone who is a knockout. You have seen, many times, the natural facial expression that enhances the sign for "beautiful." Try to envision that specific facial expression, the one where the man meets the woman or vice versa, and one or the other is smitten. You have seen many examples of this type of facial expression on television commercials, in stage performances, and in real life. For instance, you may notice stars in the eyes, rapid blinking, a dazed or dazzled look in the eye, and often a certain tilt to the head.

LOOK, SEE: Move the "V" hand forward away from your eye. This sign may be executed with one or both hands and can be moved in the direction of the person or object being "looked" at.

BEAUTIFUL: Use the "open five" hand, starting at your chin, moving clockwise in front of your face, and ending with a closed hand.

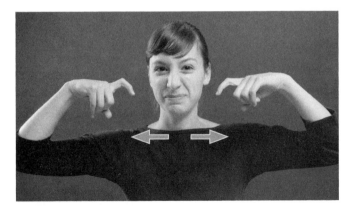

UGLY: Use both "X" hands, palms down in front of your mouth and nose, then pull quickly apart. *Variation:* To modify this sign, lessening the severity, use only one "X" hand instead of two.

CHUBBY: Place both "claw" hands on each side of your cheeks

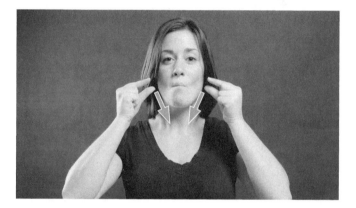

THIN: Use the "G" hand drawn down your cheeks. *Memory aid*: Think of the gaunt cheeks on a slender face. *Note*: In sign language, using the pinky handshape can represent things that are thin, like lines or spaghetti. This variation is a cute sign and requires good facial expression: Touch both pinky fingertips, palms facing in, and pull apart. Really suck in your cheeks to make them appear gaunt.

Expressing Emotions

Now let's look at how you can use sign language to describe your emotions and feelings. As you begin to learn the following signs, it is important to add appropriate facial expressions. When a feeling or emotion is strong, whether it is positive or negative, your facial expression needs to support this information.

HAPPY: Place both "flat" hands on your chest and pat with an upward movement several times and smile. Now, add a big or little smile depending on your degree of happiness. This sign, without a smile, makes you a monotone signer.

ANGRY, GROUCHY: Snap the "claw" hand tersely in front of your face. To demonstrate the degree of angry or grouchy scrunch up your face appropriately. *Variation:* To sign "grouchy," "irritable," or "annoyed," move your "claw" hand back and forth a couple of times in front of your face. Add the appropriate degree of intensity on your face to help demonstrate the difference between "angry" and "annoyed." To accomplish this, you can raise an eyebrow; if you have long hair, flip your hair back, or make a big sigh.

SAD, DEPRESSED: Drop "open five" hands down from your face. In order to have a good facial impact, you need to form the sign while dropping the head and looking sad with sincerity. If you are "depressed," drop the "open five" hands down, with middle finger extended toward your body, from shoulder to waist.

CRAZY: Circle the "claw" hand several times at the side of your head. Both hands may be used for this sign to demonstrate intensity. One of the facial expressions that can be used is to somewhat stick your tongue out of the corner of your mouth. *Variation:* To sign "crazy," or "mad about," circle the index finger several times at the temple. Both index fingers may be used for this natural gestural version. The degree of intensity depends on facial expression, such as rolling your eyes around.

PROUD: Draw the "A" hand straight up your chest. Add the appropriate body language: straight back, head up, chin out.

LONELY: Draw the index finger of the "one" hand down your chin. Add the appropriate facial by looking downward with a slightly sad face.

SMILE: Use both index fingers of the "one" hands and draw a smile up and away from your mouth. Flash a big smile while forming this sign! *Variation:* To demonstrate a large smile draw both "B" hands up and away from the mouth, imitating a "smiley face."

TIRED: To sign "tired," drop "bent" hands slightly at center of your chest and lean forward with a look of droopy eyes.

FUNNY: To sign "funny," brush the index and middle fingers off the side of your nose. This sign needs a little smile to be believable.

Using Signs in Storytelling

In this section, there are common verbs for you to learn. These general verbs are needed in storytelling and are easily applied in common everyday chatter.

COME: Move both index fingers toward you in a beckoning motion. This sign is a natural gesture.

GO: Move your index fingers away from your body. This sign is a natural gesture and can be moved in any direction.

TALK: Use both extended index fingers, palms facing, moving back and forth from your mouth. To sign "conversation," use the hand-shape of "C." This is an "initialized" sign. *Variation:* To sign "yada, yada yada," move the "four" hand back and forth from the corner of your mouth.

SLEEP: With your palm facing inward, pull down while slowly closing your hand. Close your eyes and bend down your head.

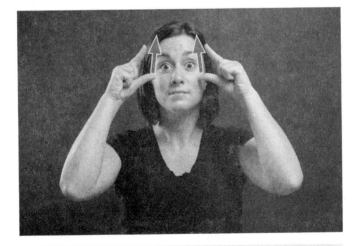

WAKE UP: Place both "G" hands at the corner of your closed eyes. Spread your index fingers and thumbs open, imitating eyes opening.

icle. You can think of this classifier as a minicar—one
around. Form this classifier on both hands and you will
Move them around and you can describe a two-car col-
and middle fingertips are the front of your minicar. In
is a detailed description of the three-finger classifier.

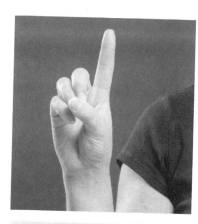

d your thumb,
middle finger. This
esent cars, boats,
, bicycles, and

Classifier 1: Extend your index "one"
finger. This classifier can represent
thin long things, such as people,
pencils, trees, sticks, poles, and lines.

RUN: Use modified "L" hands. Hold your right thumb on your left
index finger and move your hands forward quickly while flicking
your right index finger and left thumb. *Memory aid*: This handshape
is imitating a pair of feet, one in front of the other.

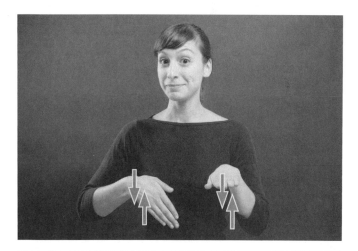

WALK: Use the "flat" hands with palms facing down, and move your
hands alternately, imitating walking.

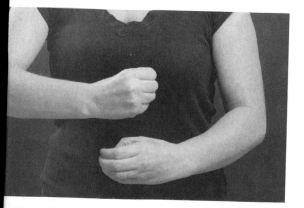

C: Form the handshape of the letter "C." This classifier can
cylindrical items, such as a glass, cup, or bottle. *Note*: When
vo hands together in the shape of "C," you can make the
any vase, pipe, or cylindrical object with a gliding movement.

You have just learned verbs. Some of these verbs are natural movements such as "come" and "go." Without thinking, you probably have already executed some of these signs in a natural gesture. The natural ease of forming and moving these signs is one of the elements that make sign language an instinctive mode of communication.

The next sign is used frequently in signed conversations. It is the sign for "understand." This sign is presented in a question form and used as "understood" for affirmation. It is used and interjected during a long story or lengthy complicated conversation. Since sign language is a visual language, you can blink, sneeze, or break eye contact for a split second and miss a sign or two, or even three. Therefore, try to remember that applying this sign for "understand" is quite important.

UNDERSTAND (both images): Place the "S" hand at your temple, palm facing back, and then snap open your index finger to a vertical position.

Classifiers

Now it's time to add yet anoth
sifiers. Classifiers give clarity,
learn many new signs. Classifi
lar palm positions. The specifi
objects and display their movem
used correctly, classifiers add e
conversation.

There are a vast number of
the surface of this subject by pr
classifiers. Each of these seven
that label can include an arrow o
ing a classifier, the signer will us
palm positions.

The name labels of seven I
handshapes:

- CL 3: Uses only "three" fing
- CL 1: Uses the extended "on
- CL C: Uses the handshape o
- CL 5: Uses the handshape of
- CL Λ: Uses the letter "V," in
- CL L: Uses the handshape of
- CL B: Uses the letter "B" (fl
  positions

These name labels are used in
ies, books, and ASL courses. Cla
tions; this is especially true when

Think of a classifier as pronou
the signer explains what the classi
alone nouns or verbs. Novice sign
first, before they apply the classifi
you can fingerspell the word, the
shape. Confused? Don't worry; fo
understand.

The three-finger classifier (CL
apply when relating a story or ev

discussing a veh
you can move al
have two cars. N
lision. The index
Chapter 6, there

Classifier 3: Exter
index finger, and
classifier can repr
trains, motorcycle
more.

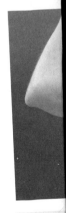

Classifie
represent
you use t
shape of

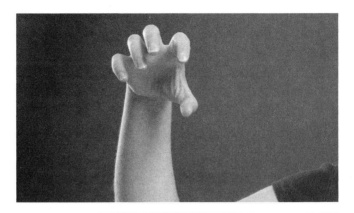

Classifier 5: Form a down-turned "claw" handshape. This classifier can represent a pile of laundry, a clump of hedges, or a mound of leaves.

Classifier Λ: Form a letter "V" with your index and middle finger and turn it upside down. This classifier represents the "legs" of a person. Swinging the fingers back and forth can represent a person walking. *Variation:* Another extended form of a classifier is a "bent V." To form, use the letter "V" with the index and middle fingers bent at the knuckles. By holding one or both hands slightly upright, this classifier can be used to demonstrate animal movement, such as a rabbit hopping, frogs leaping, lions stalking, snakes slithering, and more.

Classifier L: Form the letter "L" with both hands, your thumb tips touching. This classifier can demonstrate small rectangular things such as licenses, license plates, bricks, checks, business cards, or credit cards. *Variation:* Another extended form of a classifier is using an "L" that is bent at the first knuckle. Place your two bent "L" hands together, thumb tips touching, and this classifier can demonstrate a small saucer. Spread your hands further apart, and you can shape out a large dinner plate or platter.

The next classifier is used frequently in describing multiple objects. It represents flat objects, such as papers, walls, floors, curtains, doors, tables, windows, ceilings, shelves, and more. By manipulating the position of the CL B, or "flat" hand classifier, you can make the shape of a box, which is also the shape of a room. The "flat" hand is the most commonly used handshape; not only does it work as a classifier, it is used extensively in forming signs.

Next, you will view five images of the various palm positions that can be used when applying the CL B. These images illustrate moving the "flat" handshape into various palm positions to demonstrate windows, walls, floors, curtains, and more. The flat handshape is a powerful tool. Knowing how to move the "flat" hand classifier for visually specific information also makes it unique. This is especially true if you are redecorating and remodeling. The "flat" handshape is also a natural gesture. You have probably used this natural gesture many times when describing things, without giving it a second thought.

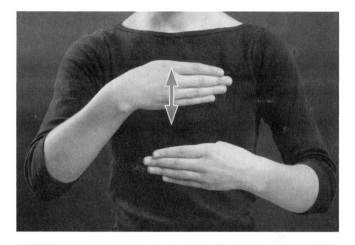

CLASSIFIER B ↕ **:** Hold both "flat" hands edge to edge. The little finger of your right hand should rest on top of your left thumb, and your palms should face inward. Move your right hand up and down to demonstrate opening and closing a window.

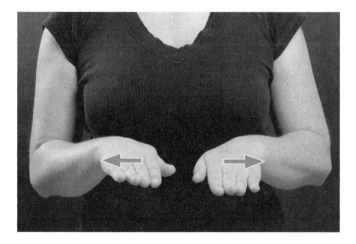

CLASSIFIER B ◄— —► **:** Hold both "flat" hands side by side, palms facing down. Separate your hands by sliding them apart. This handshape and movement demonstrates a tabletop, countertop, floor, or any basic horizontal flat surface.

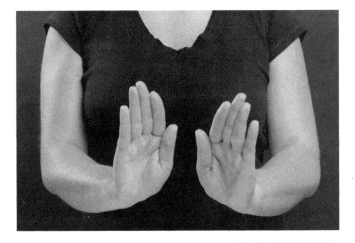

CLASSIFIER B ▼ ◄─► **:** Hold both "flat" hands side by side vertically, palms facing forward. This handshape moved in various directions can demonstrate an array of doors, such as any regular door, or sliding or swinging double doors. Move the flat handshapes downward and they can represent drapes on a window and more.

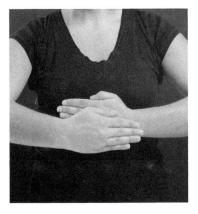

CLASSFIER B ☐ **:** Hold both "flat" hands facing each other in the first position (left image). Change to the second position, both palms facing inward with the left hand close to the body (right image). The palm positions and movements demonstrate first the sidewalls, then the front and back walls, forming a room. The movement demonstrates any item that is square, or box shaped.

Remember: When the CL B, or flat handshape, is used to describe flat objects such as walls, floors, or a room, it is called a classifier.

Shaping Language with Classifiers

This section will help you take a look at the different ways you can use those classifier handshapes. The following table shows a list of items beneath their appropriate classifier. These items can be easily pictured in your mind. Using classifiers, you can form these shapes as big or as small as you desire. You can move and arrange them anywhere within your signing space. Remember, some of these items require you to use two hands when shaping them with classifiers. Think of your hands as the tools for molding and shaping the objects.

In a set of instructions, the abbreviation "CL" is used for classifiers.

CL B Flat hand	CL 5 Claw hand	CL C "C" hand	CL L Bent "L"	CL 1 "One" hand
Box	Snowball	Glass	Plate	Tree
Table	Light bulb	Flashlight	Pizza tray	Thermometer
Book	Flowerbed	Cup	Cookie	Stripes
Floor	Bushes	Bowl	Badge	Telephone pole
Window	Rubbish	Vacuum hose	Coaster	Person
Curtains	Laundry piles	Vase	Saucer	Popsicle

Remember, a sign for every word does not exist. Using classifiers fills the gaps and adds greater visual clarity. This introduction to classifiers will give you a major advantage should you enroll in an ASL course. Don't worry about grasping all the concepts right now. The next chapter makes one of the classifiers much easier to understand by "letting your fingers do the walking."

04 / Playtime: Signing Sports and Venturing Outside

IN THIS CHAPTER, you will learn how to apply a simple classifier to show physical movements, such as walking, sitting, and dancing. You will also be introduced to vocabulary to describe your experiences in the world's natural playground: the great outdoors. Remember to have fun while you learn the subjects in this chapter.

A Helpful Classifier

A signer can show many movements by simply moving the index and middle fingers into various positions. This classifier introduced in Chapter 3 is formed by an upside down "V," and it is used to demonstrate movements or body positions. Here are some of the most common movement signs.

WALK: Make an inverted "V" with your index and middle fingers and alternately swing the fingers, imitating walking.

STAND: Use your index and middle fingers to make an inverted "V." Place the fingers onto your left open palm, imitating a pair of legs standing.

JUMP, HOP: Place the inverted "V" onto the left open palm, then pull up while bending both fingers and knuckles, imitating jumping.

STAND ON ONE LEG: Use the index and middle fingers to make an inverted "V," onto the left open palm, then pull up one finger.

KNEEL, CRAWL: To sign "kneel," place the knuckles of the inverted "V" hand onto the left open palm. To sign "crawl," alternately move the knuckles forward, imitating the movement of crawling.

It's important to get used to using the inverted "V" classifiers for many reasons, one of which is that when used by nurses and medical professionals, this classifier is extremely helpful. These professionals are able to demonstrate to patients how they need to be positioned for physical therapy, procedures, tests, examinations, or for their comfort.

LIE DOWN: Place the right "V" hand, palm down, onto your left open palm.

To sign "lie on side," place the right "V" hand onto your left palm, on the edge of either the index or middle finger, depending on which side you want to demonstrate.

To sign "roll over," place the right "V" hand, palm down, onto your left palm, then flip the "V" hand over. A cute way to demonstrate you "didn't sleep at all last night," is to make this movement several times, because you tossed and turned.

FALL: Place the inverted "V" hand onto the left open palm. Now make the "V" jump off the end of your fingers, imitating falling.

Try to be mindful of which "fall" you are signing. This is "fall" as in physically falling, and then there is a different sign for "fall" as in autumn.

DANCE: Place the inverted "V" onto the open palm, swing your hand back and forth, and kick up your "heels."

SIT: Bend the knuckles of your right inverted "V" hand over your extended left "H" hand. Visualize legs dangling over the edge of a chair.

To sign "swing," form the sign for "sit," then swing your hands back and forth, imitating sitting on a swing.

Sport Signs

In this section, you will apply the "person" ending that was introduced in Chapter 2. This is a great chance to practice your newfound knowledge. The next set of vocabulary words will be related to sports. However, you can double that vocabulary set by simply signing the sport and then transforming it to indicate the player. For instance, if you sign the word "golf" then add the "person" sign, the sign becomes "golfer."

The following images of sport signs serve a dual purpose. From them, you will learn to sign specific sports, while at the same time you will continue to learn how to form a compound sign. As mentioned before, the compound sign is made by simply adding the "person" sign immediately after signing any one of these sports signs described. Just to refresh your memory, take another look at the "person" sign in Chapter 2.

HOCKEY: Use your bent index finger to sweep across the "open" left palm, imitating a hockey stick. Add the "person" sign, and the sign becomes "hockey player."

FOOTBALL: Use both "open five" hands, palms facing each other, and interlock your fingers together several times, imitating two teams crashing together. Add the "person" sign, and now the sign becomes "football player."

As you can see, many of the sports signs are mimed or gestured. Here are a few more that are signed exactly the way you would imagine:

- To sign "baseball," hold both fists at shoulder level, imitating holding a baseball bat.
- To sign "golf," hold both fists as though you are swinging a golf club.
- To sign "swimming," move both arms, imitating a swimming stroke.
- To sign "basketball," hold an imaginary basketball and imitate the action of shooting a basket.

Add the "person" sign to each of the sports, and the sign describes a player of the sport (baseball player, golfer, swimmer, basketball player).

Additional Compound Signs

By now, you have begun to realize how you can transform the different sports signs to mean the players themselves by forming a compound sign. However, sports signs aren't the only ones you can use in compound signs. There are many compound signs in sign language. As your sign vocabulary grows, you will begin to recognize many of these types of compound signs. You have learned how easy it is to form a compound sign, which adds detail and clarity to the topic. Here are two more examples of using compound signs.

CAMERA: Hold an imaginary camera up to the eye and press the shutter button with the index finger. Remember, adding the "person" sign changes this sign to "photographer."

PAINT: To sign "paint," brush the right fingertips back and forth across the left "open" palm, imitating brush strokes. Add the "person" sign, and now the sign becomes "painter."

A Sign of the Times

A sports chapter in a sign language book would not be complete without a story about a famous deaf ballplayer. William Ellsworth "Dummy" Hoy was born in 1862. He lived to be nearly 100 years old before passing away in 1961. Hoy was the first deaf professional baseball player in the major leagues.

There are several stories surrounding Hoy and his contributions to the game of baseball. Some of these stories have been validated by newspaper clippings from as far back as 1888. In the early days of baseball, all umpire calls were shouted. It is said Hoy was responsible for the creation of the signals for "strike," "safe," and "out." Hoy created these signals because neither he nor the crowd could hear the calls by the home plate umpires. Today these signals are tradition and are used by umpires worldwide.

Some say that the intricate system of hand signals used in baseball and softball games today can be traced back to Hoy. These additional signals would include the manager's call signals to the batter, as well as the outfielders' calls.

William Hoy was one of the few players to have played in four of the five recognized major leagues, and he held an outstanding baseball career record. The crowds loved Hoy, and to show their approval, they stood in the bleachers and waved their hats and arms to demonstrate their enthusiasm. Some say this is the first early form of "deaf applause," a visual form of applauding.

DEAF APPLAUSE: Raise both hands high in the air, in an "open five" position, and shake them.

Playing Outside

The great outdoors offers a perfect sign language lesson. You can go for a walk, and while enjoying the fresh air you can see and practice what you have just learned. This chapter will introduce you to the signs for different animals, weather, and some of nature's finest elements.

The Animal Kingdom

Animal signs are a delight to learn, as they are often iconic. In this section, you have the opportunity to apply the classifiers that you have just learned and combine them with this new group of sign vocabulary. After studying the new vocabulary, you will be able to use classifiers as an enhancer, giving you a wonderful way to show movement. As an example, you can combine the classifier for animal movement (a bent "V" hand) with the animal sign for "lion." This combination of a classifier and a sign demonstrates that the lion is moving. When you use this classifier slowly, you can suggest the appearance of a lion crouching. Add the sign for "tree," which you will also find in this section. Now, simply pluralize tree by signing it multiple times. Voila! You have just added a jungle.

ANIMAL: Place the fingertips of both hands on your chest and rock the hands back and forth, imitating an animal breathing.

LION: Pull the "claw" hand back over your head, imitating a lion's enormous mane.

TIGER: Use both "claw" hands placed on both sides of your cheeks and draw them apart several times, imitating a tiger's stripes.

BEAR: Use "claw" hands and cross your arms on your chest, moving the hands to imitate clawing.

RABBIT: Place the "three" hands on both sides of your head, palms facing back. Flick your fingers and thumb repeatedly, imitating the ears. The "flat" hand held in the same position can be used for very young children. *Variation:* Use the "H" hands, cross wrists, palms facing in, in front of your chest. Flick your fingers repeatedly.

CAT: Pull the "F" hands from the corners of your mouth to the sides, imitating a cat's whiskers.

COW: Place the thumb of both "Y" hands at your temple and twist, imitating the cow's horns. Good signers use two hands for children which adds strong visuals to stories and use just one hand with adults. *Note*: Make this sign with two hands and it will add animation.

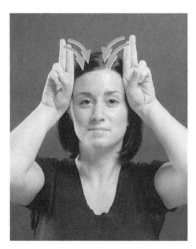

HORSE: Place the "H" hands, palms forward, on your head and flick your fingers.

Signing bird, duck, and goose can be an adventure in learning sizes for a young child. Sign a small beak for a bird, a medium beak for duck, and a large beak for goose.

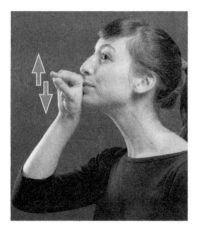

BIRD: Open and close your index finger and thumb at the side of your mouth, representing a small beak.

To sign "duck," open and close your index finger, middle finger, and thumb at the side of your mouth, representing a medium-size beak.

To sign "goose," open and close your thumb and all fingers at the side of your mouth, representing a large beak.

WOLF: Place a slightly open hand over your nose and pull down, while closing your hand, to the end, imitating the long nose of a wolf.

SKUNK: Place the "K" hand at the bridge of your nose and pull back over your head, imitating the white stripe on a skunk.

RACCOON: Place both "V" hands, palms inward, at your eyes, and pull out to the sides, closing your fingers, imitating the mask of a raccoon.

SQUIRREL: Hold both hands upright in front of your chest with heels touching and tap the fingertips of both bent "V" hands several times, imitating the squirrel's gnawing.

SNAKE: To sign "snake," move the bent "V" hand forward in a winding movement, imitating a snake.

DEER: Place the thumbs of both "open five" hands at your temples, imitating antlers.

To sign "moose," make the sign for "deer" and pull out the "open five" hands away from the side of the head, imitating the large antlers on a moose.

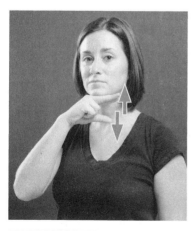

FROG: Place your closed fist under your chin, flick open your index and middle fingers, imitating the frog's throat.

TURTLE: Place the "A" hand, palm facing left, under the "curved" left hand. Move the thumb of your "A" hand back and forth under the left curved hand, imitating the head of a turtle inside its shell.

To sign "sea turtle," place the right fist on top of the left fist, fully extend both thumbs. Rotate both thumbs simultaneously, imitating a sea turtle swimming.

To sign "manta ray," place the right "flat" hand on top of the left "flat" hand, extend thumbs and move them back and forth, while moving hands forward in a slight wavy motion.

DINOSAUR: Hold your right arm vertical, palm facing left. Rest your elbow on the back of the fingertips of your left horizontal arm. Use the flattened "O" hand and pivot your wrist back and forth slowly, imitating the swaying head of a dinosaur.

BUG: Place the tip of your thumb on the tip of your nose and wiggle the bent index and middle fingers, imitating antennae on a bug.

SPIDER: To sign "spider," cross both "open five" hands at the wrist and wiggle your fingers while moving forward, imitating a spider crawling.

The Elements

The morning news comes on, and the weatherperson announces it is going to be cold today. There will be rain with lightning and thunder. There is even a possibility of the weather changing to snow. A family member is flying out the door, and you want to warn her of the change in the weather pattern.

In just a moment, you will be able to sign this from the doorway as she is getting in the car.

WEATHER: Use the "W" hands, palms facing. Twist your hands in opposite directions twice. This sign represents the ever-changing weather patterns.

SNOW: Wiggle the fingers of the "open five" hands, dropping your hands down several times, imitating falling snowflakes.

In Chapter 1 you were introduced to the sign for "rain." You can change "rain" to "snow" just by wiggling your fingers.

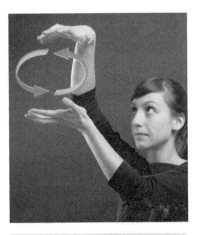

LIGHTNING: Use your index finger and trace a downward zigzag movement, imitating a lightning bolt.

CLOUD, FOG: Make a swirling motion with both "claw" hands above your head for "cloud." The sign for "fog" is similar to the "cloud" sign, except it's formed about waist high. This makes perfect sense: clouds are in the sky, and fog is near the ground.

THUNDER: Tap both "A" hands alternately against your chest. You can feel the rumble in your body.

WIND, BREEZE: Sweep the "open five" hands side to side in front of your body. The intensity with which you move your hands back and forth in front of your body will indicate the wind's gentleness or its ferocity.

SUN: Use your index finger and form a clockwise circle above the right side of your head. *Variation:* To sign "sunshine," sign "sun," then form a wide "open five" to show the rays of the sun.

SKY: Using both "flat" hands, palms facing, cross your arms in front of your body above your head in an arched movement and spread your arms open. *Variation:* This sign can be formed using one "curved" hand forming a large arc from left to right above the head.

Exploring Nature

Nature's vast and wonderful world is filled with amazing creatures and natural beauty. Sign language, with its iconic elements, reflects some of this beauty. If you are a nature lover or photographer, or if you just like to walk in the woods, you will appreciate these signs.

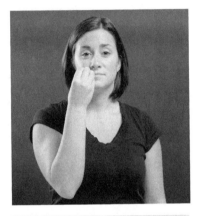

TREE: Hold your right arm vertical and rest the elbow on the back of the fingertips of the hand of the left horizontal arm. Using an "open five" hand, palm facing forward, pivot your wrist back and forth repeatedly.

FLOWER: Gently tap the "O" hand under your right nostril and then the left. This sign and movement imitates smelling flowers. Form this sign with an "R" hand and you are signing "Rose."

To form "forest/jungle" repeat the formation while moving the arm right to left, imitating many trees.

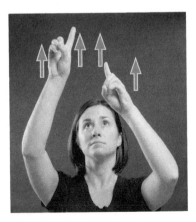

STARS: Point both index fingers upward and move your fingers alternately skyward.

RAINBOW: Hold the left "four" hand vertical, then sweep your right "four" hand left to right in an arc above your head, demonstrating the colors and shape in the sky.

OCEAN: Move both your "curved" hands forward, palms down, with one hand slightly behind the other, imitating rolling waves on the ocean.

BEACH: Begin with your elbow resting on the back of your left hand, held in front of the body. Brush the outside edge of your left arm with your "flat" right hand several times.

This sign for "beach" allows the signer to show gentle or ferocious surf. This sign can also demonstrate high tide by sweeping the right hand high above the arm or low tide by sweeping outward and down below the arm.

In this chapter, there have been many beautiful signs. Explore putting together signs to create short sentences. Your sign vocabulary is building. Signs from earlier chapters would help create sentences, such as "The sky is beautiful." "I am happy to see the sun." Keep in mind, the small words such as "the" and "is" do not need to be signed.

05 / Learning Numbers and Signing Time

THIS CHAPTER WILL introduce simple numbers and give you a guideline to master the basic formations. You will learn to form signed numbers with ease and quickly be counting up to a million on one hand. Along the way, you'll also learn how to sign fractions and signs related to money. This chapter will also introduce you to many of the common "time" signs. You will quickly learn the months of the year and their fingerspelled abbreviations. There will also be seasons and holiday signs to add to your new sign vocabulary.

It's All in the Numbers

You use many different kinds of numbers in your daily conversation. For instance, a conversation might include a phone number, credit card number, model number, and so forth. Now it's time for you to learn how to use numbers in ASL.

Unfortunately, a novice signer often feels that numbers are confusing and somewhat complicated. In order to minimize confusion, this chapter will take a look at examples of numbers that seem to be the pitfalls for new signers. These particular numbers are the ones that share the same handshapes as the letters of the alphabet, thus causing the confusion. Don't become discouraged. There are only a few of these numbers, and there will be a guide for you. The context of a conversation generally adds the clarity that is needed to distinguish between a signed number and letter.

It's important to keep in mind that the way numbers are signed can vary according to region. In some regions, the numbers are signed with the palms facing you; in others, the palm is facing the reader. Don't let this worry you. Both palm positions are correct, depending on your geographical region and perhaps on your ASL teacher as well.

Your flexibility as a new signer really counts in this chapter. Tips and visual examples are right here to support you. Now, warm up your fingers and wrists and get ready to count to ten.

Counting to Ten

Counting to ten is easy. You have been doing this since you were a child. In this case, however, there is one little difference. When you were a child, you had to use two hands to count this high. In sign language, you can count to ten (and much higher) using just one hand! A nice starting place for the material covered in this chapter is to learn to sign "number," and the sign for "0" (zero).

NUMBER: Touch the fingertips of both flattened "O" hands, and pivot back and forth alternately.

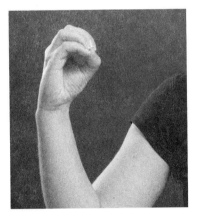

ZERO: Form the letter "O," palm facing left.

The sign for the number "0" will be used in forming other numbers.

One Through Five

Now you can begin the simple task of counting to ten. The ASL form for counting is just a little different from the way you counted to ten as a child. With a quick look at the images, you should be able to duplicate the individual handshape of numbers "1" through "5" without any problems. Keep in mind that the number "3" requires the vertical extension of your thumb along with your index and middle fingers. The handshape for the number "5" is referred to as the "open five."

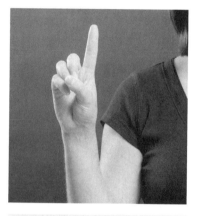

ONE: Hold your index finger upright in the vertical position, palm forward, all other fingers tucked away.

TWO: Hold your index and middle fingers slightly spread apart, upright in the vertical position, palm forward, all other fingers tucked away.

THREE: Hold your index finger, middle finger, and thumb slightly spread apart, upright in the vertical position, palm forward, all other fingers tucked away.

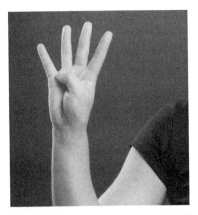

FOUR: Hold your index, middle, ring, and pinky fingers slightly spread apart, upright in the vertical position, palm forward, and thumb tucked into the palm.

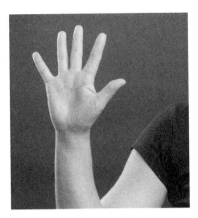

FIVE: Hold all fingers spread apart, upright in the vertical position, palm forward.

Six Through Ten

The counting process changes for six through nine. It's easy; you only need to touch a specific finger to your thumb. Remember, to hold the remaining fingers upright, and have your palm facing forward. Just think, there is no need to use both hands to count above five again!

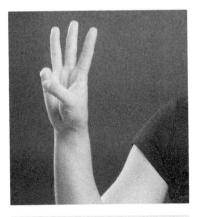

SIX: Touch your pinky finger to your thumb.

SEVEN: Touch your ring finger to your thumb.

If you're thinking that the number "6" looks like the letter "W," you're right. Remember, the context of a signed conversation will help you to differentiate between numbers and letters.

EIGHT: Touch your middle finger to your thumb.

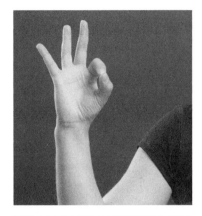

NINE: Touch your index finger to your thumb.

If you're thinking that the number "9" is another example of duplicity, you're right again. It has the same handshape as the letter "F."

TEN: Extend your thumb on the "A" hand and pivot your wrist to the right.

Time to Review

You made it to ten counting on one hand! Let's do a quick review of how you accomplished this. In sign language, the pinky finger represents the number "6." The ring finger represents the number "7." The middle finger represents the number "8." The index finger represents the number "9." When you lightly touch any of these four fingers separately to the thumb, this action confirms the number position. Simply refer to this table until you master the numbers.

Number	Finger Position
6	pinky
7	ring
8	middle
9	index
10	thumb

Here is another memory aid to help you: Little finger, little number; big finger, big number.

Now, let's examine those numbers and letters that share the same handshapes and that are the cause of some confusion for novice signers:

- The number "2" is formed in the same way as the letter "V."
- The number "6" is formed in the same way as the letter "W."
- The number "9" is formed in the same way as the letter "F."
- The number "10" is formed in the same way as the letter "A," but with the addition of a twist of the wrist.

Number Handshapes as Descriptors

You will find that the handshapes of numbers are also used as descriptors. Instructions in sign language dictionaries often refer to numbers to describe handshapes. For example, you may see entries that tell you to use the "one" hand or to use the "three" hand. In previous pages of this book, you have already read instructions on forming a sign that used the handshape of a number: an "open five" hand. Knowing how to form all the handshapes, including numbers, is a very important part of your new journey into this visual language.

Conversations with Letters and Numbers

When a conversation occurs that requires both letters and numbers, such as a password or an e-mail address, the dilemma can be resolved in two easy ways. The first solution is to slightly shake the numbers back and forth while maintaining a smooth flow for the letters. This slight movement helps to establish that you are signing a number and not a letter. The second solution is to sign all numbers with the palm facing you and all letters with the palm facing the reader. Of these two methods, the first one, shaking the numbers, is the easiest for the novice signer.

Eleven Through Nineteen

Now it's time to move on and learn the next section of numbers. As a memory guide to help you along, the numbers "11" through "15" will be referred to as the "flicks." (You'll see why in just a moment.) Look back at the images of "1" through "5" and set them in your mind. The reason; numbers "11" to "15" use the same handshapes as numbers "1" through "5."

Now, one at time, form the same handshapes for each number and simply "flick" the appropriate fingers *twice*. These numbers are formed with the *palm facing you*. The index finger is flicked for eleven. The index and middle finger are flicked for twelve. Continue to do the same right through fifteen. It's easy!

ELEVEN: With your palm facing you, flick your index finger twice.

- To sign "12," palm facing you, flick your index and middle fingers twice.
- To sign "13," palm facing you, flick your thumb, index, and middle fingers twice.
- To sign "14," palm facing you, flick your index, middle, ring, and pinky fingers twice.
- To sign "15," palm facing you, flick the "open five" hand.

Moving right along, let's take on numbers "16" through "19," which are referred to as the "swing-outs." The good news is that the finger positions for numbers that contain a "6" through "9" remain constant. These numbers begin with the palm facing you and then swing out to the right ending with the palm facing forward. Forming the number "16" begins by touching the thumb to the pinky, palm facing you, then swinging out to face the receiver. The numbers "17" through "19" are formed in the same manner, by first touching your thumb to the appropriate fingers then swinging out. There is a variation in signing "16" through "19." Some people form these number signs by starting with signing the number "10" then adding a "6," "7," "8," or "9."

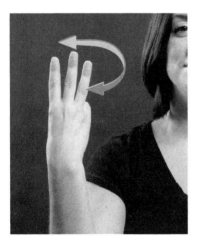

SIXTEEN: Touch your thumb to your pinky, palm facing you, then swing your hand out to the right, ending with palm forward.

- To sign "17," touch your thumb to your ring finger, palm facing you, then swing your hand out to the right, ending with palm forward.
- To sign "18," touch your thumb to your middle finger, palm facing you, then swing your hand out to the right, ending with palm forward.

■ To sign "19," touch your thumb to your index finger, palm facing you, then swing your hand out to the right, ending with palm forward.

Keep in mind that these instructions have been simplified in order to give you a survival guide to signing numbers. When you journey further into your studies of sign language, you will be exposed to a multitude of variations when it comes to signing numbers. Nonetheless, by mastering the basics shown in this chapter, you will have a wonderful head start.

Counting to Ninety

You made it through two whole sets of numbers! To reward you for all your hard work, we'll now finish off with the easier numbers.

Twenty: Use your index finger and thumb only, all other fingers tucked away. Bring your index finger and thumb together while slightly pulling back.

The sign for "20" is a standalone sign. In order to form the handshapes for the numbers "30," "40," "50," "60," "70," "80," and "90," you will need to sign the basic number first, such as "3," "4," or "5." You will then sign a "0" (zero).

A memory aid for these numbers is an easy formula: The number then changes to zero. Take a look at the following image.

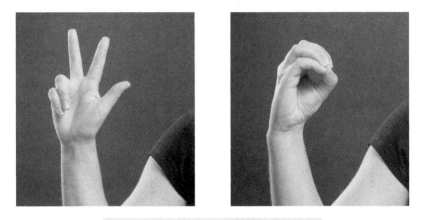

THIRTY: Sign the number "3," then a zero, "0."

- To sign "40," sign the number "4," then "0."
- To sign "50," sign the number "5," then "0."
- To sign "60," sign the number "6," then "0."
- To sign "70," sign the number "7," then "0."
- To sign "80," sign the number "8," then "0."
- To sign "90," sign the number "9," then "0."

If you take your sign language studies further, such as enrolling in a sign language course, you will learn that there are a few shortcuts to numbers. However, for now, all you need is to master the basic numbers.

Higher Numbers and Fractions

You have made it all the way up to "99." Now you will begin working on large numbers. The big numbers—hundreds, thousands, millions—require the simple application of modified Roman numerals. These signs are compound signs. The letter "C" represents the Roman numeral for "hundred." Whenever you want to sign a number in the hundreds, you form the number, then add the letter "C." For example, if you sign "1" and then the letter "C," this equals "100." You can continue in the same pattern for "200," "300," "400," and so on.

A good memory aid: A hundred-dollar bill is often referred to as a "C note."

HUNDRED: Place the letter "C" in the left palm.

To sign the number "100," sign the number "1," then the letter "C," into the palm of your hand.

The letter "M" represents the Roman numeral for "thousand." Whenever you want to sign a number in the thousands, you form the number and add the letter "M." It is the same pattern that you just used for forming numbers in the hundreds.

THOUSAND: Tap the extended fingers of the letter "M" once in your left palm.

A "million" is signed by tapping the letter "M" twice in the palm.

Fractions

While the thought of fractions may make you groan, the good news is that they are very easy to sign. They are signed exactly the way they appear, one number over the other. First sign the top number, the numerator, followed by the bottom number, the denominator.

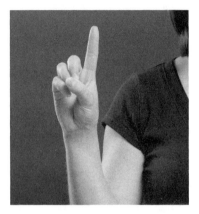 

ONE-HALF: Form the handshape "1," move hand down slightly and change to the handshape of "2."

You have created the visual of a "1" above a "2" and this visual demonstrates a numeric fraction. Use this same pattern and order of signs for all fractions.

Money and Shopping

Now it's time to combine your basic numbers with money-related signs. Everyone likes to have money, and the first sign indicates that money is in your hand.

MONEY: To sign "money," tap the back of the modified "O" hand on your left palm several times.

RICH: First sign "money," then change the handshape to a down-turned "claw" hand, and pull up, representing a stack of money. The higher you raise the stack, the richer you are. This sign is another example of a compound sign.

BANK: Slide the right "B" hand, palm up, between the thumb and palm of the down-turned left "B" hand. Hint: Visualize sliding a deposit envelope into an ATM machine.

POOR: Place the "open five" hand on your elbow and pull down to a modified "O." Visualize holes in your elbow sleeve.

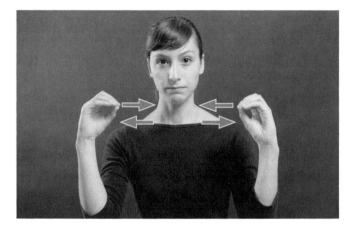

NONE: Use both hands, form the sign for "0" (zero), move hands apart. This movement can be made several times to show degree of emphasis.

SELL, SALE: Use the modified "O," bend both wrists downward and pivot forward once.

To sign "shop" or "store," use the modified "O," bend both wrists downward and pivot back and forth with a double motion.

A cute memory aid for "shopping" is to imagine carrying bags, and they are swinging back and forth. The following are more helpful terms.

PROFIT: Move the "F" hand down over your heart, imitating placing money in a pocket.

TAX, COST, PRICE: Sharply draw the "X" hand down your left palm.

OWE: Tap the tip of your index finger into your left palm several times.

PAY: Place your index finger on your left palm, snap the index finger off the palm pointing forward or directionally. *Variation:* Slide the "P" hand off the left palm.

DOLLAR: Grasp the fingers of your palm-up left hand with your right hand and pull away.

Signing Everyday Numbers

Numbers fill your daily life. To help manage all those numbers, an easy rule to follow is to sign numbers exactly the way they are spoken. When you want to tell someone your phone number, you will sign numbers in groups as they are written. Phone numbers are grouped with the area code first, followed by three numbers, then by four numbers. To sign your phone number, simply hesitate just a bit in between each group of numbers: "555" (hesitate), "555" (hesitate), "5555." Don't drop your hands; just hesitate.

Here is an example of the three different ways you could sign the number "1,900."

1. When referring to "1900" as "nineteen hundred," sign "19," followed by the letter "C," representing the Roman numeral for 100.
2. When signing "1900" to represent "one thousand nine hundred," sign "1," followed by "M," representing the Roman numeral for 1,000, then "9," followed by "C." Memory aid: Numbers are signed the way you say them.
3. When signing "1900" to represent "nineteen dollars" (or $19.00), sign "19" then "dollars." You can also sign "money" or "dollar" first, then "19."

Often, when discussing money in an ASL conversation, you will see "dollar" signed first, followed by the amount. This may sound strange, but look at how you actually write dollar amounts: $19.00. You always write the dollar sign first, so it's not so strange after all!

Past, Present, and Future

The subject of time is part of our everyday conversations. There are a few easy-to-follow rules to use when signing units of time. These rules have been created to add clarity to a signed conversation. One of these rules governs when a signer should apply a "time" sign. The rule is simple: Always sign the time element *first* when relating a story or an event. For example, if you were describing last year's vacation you would sign "past year" first, then describe your vacation. In conversations using "now," "yesterday," and "tomorrow," the signer needs only to sign the time element once unless there is a change in the conversation of the time being discussed.

Now, try to imagine a physical timeline that goes straight through your body, extending out in front and back behind you. This imaginary line in front and back of you is there to represent the future and the past. All signs indicating the future are made in a forward movement and are out ahead of your body. Signs indicating the past are made with a backward movement and are pushed behind your shoulder. Therefore, the rule is: The future moves forward, and the past moves backward.

As you can see from the images, signs relating to the future are clearly indicated with a forward-moving arrow. The further you move your arm and hand forward, the further the date is in the future. In reverse, the same applies to signs relating to the past.

FUTURE: Use the "flat" hand, palm facing left. Move it forward and down.

TOMORROW: Use the "A" hand on your cheek, and turn it forward and down.

PAST: Hold the "flat" hand palm inward and push it over your shoulder.

YESTERDAY: Use the "Y" or modified "A" hand on your cheek and turn it backward.

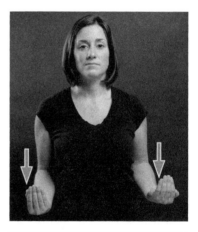

NOW, PRESENT: The "now" or "present" sign has two variations. It can also be formed using the "bent" or "Y" hands coming down in front and alongside the body. In the timeline, your body is the very center, indicating that you are standing in the "present/now" time. The sign used to indicate the "present" is formed just in front and alongside of your body.

Signing a Specific Time

Another way of indicating time is to simply point to your watch. When indicating a specific time, point to the watch, sign the correct number for the time, and then point again to the watch. To the receiver/reader, it would look like this: time, number, time. Earlier in this chapter, you learned how to form the signs for numbers. When indicating time on a clock or watch, you will need to combine number signs. It is important to make sure that you learn and remember all of the basic signs for time, as they are used frequently in a signed conversation.

TIME: Tap the top of the wrist twice, imitating tapping a watch.

MINUTE: Place the "one" hand on your left-facing vertical palm. Move your index finger forward, imitating the hands ticking on a clock.

HOUR: Place the "one" hand on your left-facing vertical palm. Rotate your index finger forward one turn, imitating one hour on the face of a clock.

General Times

Time signs play an important role in conversation. They serve to clarify when an event happened or when it will occur. These signs also assist in indicating verb tenses, when needed.

Moving on within the time elements, the three signs—morning, noon, and night—are iconic in their compositions. The position of the arms for these signs relates closely to the sun's movements as it rises and sets. When holding your left arm stationary in front of you, imagine your arm to be the horizon. The sun comes peeking over the horizon in the morning. At noon, the sun shines down from directly overhead, and at night, the sun disappears again down below the horizon.

DAY: Hold your right arm vertical, palm facing left. Rest your right elbow on the back of the fingertips of your left arm. Bring the right arm slowly down to rest on the left arm. *Variation:* This sign can be made with either the "flat" hand or the "D" hand.

LATE, NOT YET: Place the "flat" hand near your waist, palm facing back, and push back.

ONCE IN AWHILE, SOMETIMES: To sign "once in awhile" or "sometimes," swipe the index finger of your "one" hand on your left palm twice.

YEAR: Circle your right "S" hand forward and around your left "S" hand, and rest it on the top of your left hand.

NEVER: Move the "flat" hand, palm facing left, in a downward movement in the shape of a question mark.

Learning the Calendar

Using the alphabet, fingerspell the months of the year. Each month has an abbreviation. The abbreviated form is the preferred way when used in a signed conversation. Your signing skills will be strengthened when you see these abbreviations as a whole word. Seeing an abbreviated sign as a whole sign means you aren't looking to read each letter, but rather you are seeing the shape of the whole sign. This skill is an important part of beginning to recognize initialized and loan signs. It is a skill that takes time to master and that will require patience on your part. Here are a few practice tips. Look at the shape that the abbreviation creates rather than the individual letters. It is always a good idea to stretch and flex your hands before fingerspelling for any length if time, as when practicing a list of words.

Abbreviation	Word
J-A-N	January
F-E-B	February
M-A-R	March
A-P-R	April
M-A-Y	May
J-U-N	June
J-U-L	July
A-U-G	August
S-E-P-T	September
O-C-T	October
N-O-V	November
D-E-C	December

Variation: Any month with five letters or less can be fingerspelled in its entirety.

The next thing you need to learn is the days of the week. Once again, you will borrow from the alphabet and "initialize" nearly all the days of the week. There are three well-known variations in making the signs for the days of the week. These variations, which are only in the movement, are the result of regional and geographical differences. Here are the different ways these signs are made:

MONDAY FIRST *Variation:* The palm is facing you and your arm moves in a small circle, as if swinging a lasso.

MONDAY SECOND *Variation:* The palm is facing you and your arm moves in a small circle, counterclockwise.

MONDAY THIRD *Variation:* The palm faces the reader/receiver and moves in a clockwise motion.

These three variations are used throughout the country, and it is best that you are familiar with all three. However, following the rules of finger-spelling, which says the palm must face the reader/receiver, the following chart gives you instructions for the *third* variation.

Day	Sign Direction
Monday	Use the "M" hand, and rotate in a small clockwise circle.
Tuesday	Use the "T" hand, and rotate in a small clockwise circle.
Wednesday	Use the "W" hand, and rotate in a small clockwise circle.
Thursday	Use the "H" hand, and rotate in a small clockwise circle.
Friday	Use the "F" hand, and rotate in a small clockwise circle.
Saturday	Use the "S" hand, and rotate in a small clockwise circle.

Signing "Sunday" is a little different.

SUNDAY: Use the "open five" hands, with your palms forward, move your hands in opposite circular motions.

It is easy to remember how to sign the days of the week because you are simply initializing the first letter. There are only two small exceptions. Thursday uses the letter "H" because we have already used "T" for Tuesday, and Sunday is not an initialized sign at all. Instead, the sign represents a "wonderful" day.

Time to Celebrate

In this section, you will learn how to sign the seasons, as well as a few of the holidays appropriate to the seasons. Visualizing seasonal changes that occur in nature will help you memorize how to form the signs for the seasons. For instance, during the summer it is very hot, so visualize what happens when you are perspiring. You need to wipe the sweat off your brow when forming this sign. During the winter, you are feeling cold and shivering. In the springtime, the flowers push up through the ground to bloom, and fall brings the leaves floating down to the ground. The images that follow resemble these descriptions.

SUMMER: Use a "bent" index finger and drag it across the forehead.

WINTER: Shake the "S" hands while holding your arms against the body and imitate shivering. *Memory aid:* It is cold outside, and this makes you shiver. Think of feeling cold when forming this sign. This sign is also used for "cold." *Variation:* Another way to sign winter is to shake the "W" hands in the same manner while shivering.

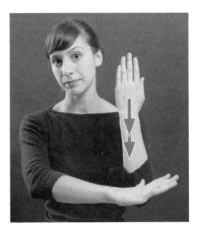

SPRING, GROW: Push your right hand up through the "open" left hand. This sign represents the growth that occurs during spring.

FALL, AUTUMN: Hold your left arm out, slightly tilted to the right, palm facing inward. Stroke the right slightly "open five" hand down along the left forearm to the elbow, imitating leaves tumbling or a barren tree.

FALL *Variation:* Use both "open five" hands, palms facing down. Start high, and float your "open five" hands side to side while moving downward, imitating leaves falling.

There are two days in spring that have special meaning for many people: Mother's Day and Father's Day. You have already learned the signs for "mother" and "father," and you just finished learning the sign for "day." Simply combine these signs.

Valentine's Day is one of the special days celebrated in many different fashions. You have already learned the "I love you" sign, and the sign for "love." Now you have two ways to say "love" to your significant other on Valentine's Day.

VALENTINE'S DAY: Use both "V" hands to outline the shape of your heart on your chest. This is an initialized sign.

THANKSGIVING: Bring the fingertips of the right and left "flat" hands from the lip area with a double forward movement. This sign for Thanksgiving is derived from the sign for "thank you" which has only one forward movement. *Variation:* Shake and lower the "Q" hand under your chin, indicating the turkey's wattle.

The sign for "Hanukkah" is made by representing the eight lit candles of the menorah.

HANUKKAH: Position the "four" hands side by side with palms facing you. Separate both hands simultaneously to the sides in a small upward arc. *Variation:* Position the "four" hands side by side with palms facing forward. Separate both hands simultaneously to the sides in a small upward arc.

Sign Variations

As you have learned, signs can be formed in more than one way and have various representations. These variations occur for several reasons—regional, geographical, the result of progress and technology, and at times, cultural or religious reasons. This chapter is a small representation of the many variations of signs within this visual language.

For example, the sign for Christmas has twelve variations, and the sign for Santa has fifteen. The sign you would select to represent Christmas or Santa may depend on where you live as well as on your specific beliefs.

- Christmas: Form an arcing "C" that moves left to right in front of the body, representing half a wreath.
- Christmas Tree: First form the sign for Christmas, then using both "flat" hands mime the shape of a Christmas tree.
- Santa Claus: Form Santa's large imaginary beard with both "C" hands, then move both hands downward to mime Santa's large belly.

SANTA: Using both "curved five" hands, mime Santa's large beard.

A good signer should always stay flexible and understand there will always be differences within ASL. Additionally, a good signer is one who learns many variations of a sign, and is familiar with a wide range of choices in forming signs.

06 / Essential Vocabulary for Home and Abroad

IN THIS CHAPTER you'll learn critical vocabulary for signing things in your home, office, and abroad. You'll also become familiar with signs for something it's crucial to communicate clearly about: Food! This chapter will broaden your ability to communicate through ASL as you branch out into the world and become more confident interacting with others through sign language.

Beginning the Day: Breakfast

It's time to eat. You need to look at food selections and plan the menu for the day. You can start with breakfast, then move on to lunch, dinner, and, of course, dessert. Along with learning the signs for foods, signs are also presented for cooking techniques and for the other items found in and around the kitchen.

HUNGRY: Draw the "C" hand down the center of your chest once, imitating a hollow feeling. *Note*: This sign is also used for the interpersonal sign of "desire."

FOOD, EAT: To sign "food," tap your lips with the modified "O" hand in a bouncy movement, imitating eating. To sign "eat," do the same but with a much more steady movement.

You learned in Chapter 5 how to make the various signs that represent time. In this chapter, you will combine these time signs with other signs. Take a moment and review how to form "morning," "noon/afternoon," and "evening/night." In the *morning*, a person *eats* breakfast, and this is exactly the description in ASL. To sign "breakfast" first sign "morning" and continue to move your hand up to the lips to sign "eat." Or, gently tap your chin with the side of your "B" hand facing left. This version is an initialized sign.

The day gets off to a better start with a good breakfast. Would you like to have bacon and eggs? These menu selections can be served with toast, a little jam or jelly, and a banana. Of course, what would the morning be without coffee and orange juice? Here are the signs for these breakfast selections:

EGGS: Strike the edges of both "H" hands together, then slightly spread them apart, imitating breaking an egg.

BACON: To sign "bacon," touch the tips of both "U" hands, palms down, and draw them apart with a wiggle, imitating bacon sizzling in a pan.

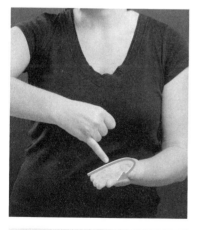

JAM, JELLY: Trace the letter "J" into the left "open" palm, imitating spreading jelly.

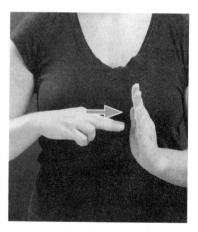

TOAST: Hold the left "flat" hand, palm facing right. Tap the right "V" hand into your palm, and on the back of your left hand. *Visualize*: You are toasting both the top and bottom of a slice of bread by tapping the "V" on *both* sides of the "flat" hand.

BANANA: Hold your left index finger upright and use your right hand to imitate the motion of peeling a banana.

COFFEE: Form the handshape of "C" with left hand, and rotate the right "S" hand counterclockwise above the left hand. *Visualize*: Turning the handle of a coffee grinder above your imaginary cup.

Chapter 3 demonstrated the color of "orange" by squeezing an "O" on your cheek. To sign "orange juice" you will need to make a very small modification: squeeze the "S" hand near the corner of your mouth or in front of your mouth.

Lunchtime!

Now it's time to learn the foods you eat at noontime, otherwise known as lunch. "Lunch" is signed in the same manner that you just signed "breakfast." To sign "lunch," form the sign for "noon" and then sign "eat."

A variation would be to gently tap the mouth using the "L" hand. This version is an initialized sign.

For lunch you could have a few light selections, such as soup and a sandwich, or a nice healthy salad with a cold glass of milk.

But then again, you could always slip away to one of those fast-food restaurants! To sign "restaurant" tap the "R" hand once on each corner of your mouth. Here, you could order a mouthwatering hamburger with cheese, tomato, onion, and mayonnaise, and a large soda. Of course, you will also have to have that extra-large order of French fries.

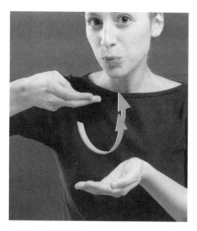

SOUP: Scoop the right "H" hand, curved like a spoon, into the curved left palm. Bring your right hand a few times up to your mouth. *Visualize*: Holding a bowl in your left hand while your right hand acts as your spoon.

SANDWICH: Bring the "flat" hands toward your mouth, imitating eating a sandwich.

SALAD: Move both "claw" hands, palms facing upward, and imitate tossing a salad in a bowl with your hands.

MILK: Squeeze one or both "S" hands alternately up and down imitating milking a cow. Often, this sign is formed using just one hand.

Signing "hamburger" is easy! It is a natural sign that imitates making a hamburger patty. Clasp both "curved" hands, as if you were making a hamburger patty, and then reverse direction.

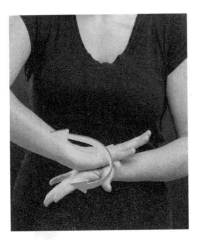

CHEESE: Press the heels of both hands together, twisting back and forth, imitating pressing cheese.

When signing condiments or dressings that are spread on bread or rolls, you form the sign by imitating a spreading motion, on the "flat" palm drawn toward you. You need only to change the handshapes for the specific item.

BUTTER: Draw the extended fingers of the right "N" hand across the left "open" palm, imitating spreading butter.

- To sign "mayonnaise," draw the extended fingers of the "M" hand across your left "open" palm, imitating spreading mayonnaise.
- To sign "mustard," circle the extended fingers of the "M" hand on your left "open" palm, imitating squirting mustard on bread.

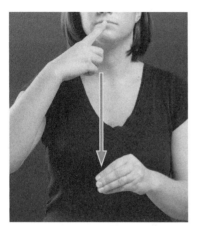

TOMATO: First sign "red," then use your right index finger to strike the left fingertips of the modified "O" hand. *Note:* This is a compound sign. Visualize holding a tomato and slicing it.

ONION: Twist the knuckle of the "X" hand in the corner of your eye. *Visualize:* Onions make you cry.

To sign "French fries," slide the "F" hand to the right in two small movements in the fingerspelling position.

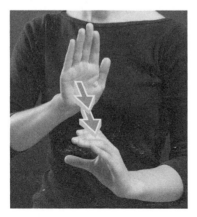

KETCHUP: With your left "C" hand, hold an imaginary "ketchup" bottle upside down. Strike the bottom of the "bottle" with the heel of the right "open five" hand. *Variation:* Shake the "K" hand up and down. This version is an initialized sign, and one of many ways to sign "ketchup."

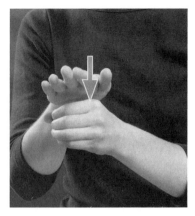

SODA: Hold an imaginary can in your left hand and hit the top of the "can" with your right hand, imitating a "pop" sound. *Variation:* Holding the imaginary can with the left hand, the right middle finger is pushed into the can, and then the hand hits the top of the can. Another variation is to pull the ring of the can before the hand hits the top of the can.

Afternoon Snack

It is late afternoon, the low point of the day. You have been working hard, and you deserve a little break. It's time for tea, cookies, or fruit. On the other hand, perhaps you want a piece of candy!

TEA: Hold an imaginary cup with your left hand and dip the "F" hand in and out, imitating dipping a tea bag.

COOKIE: Twist the "C" hand's fingertips back and forth on your left "open" palm, imitating cutting out cookies.

FRUIT: To sign "fruit" twist the "F" hand near the corner of your mouth.

SWEET: Brush the fingertips of your "flat" hand downward from the corner of your mouth and chin several times.

- To sign "sugar" or "candy," brush the fingertips of your "U" hand downward from the corner of your mouth and chin several times.
- The sign for "cute" is formed by brushing the fingertips of the "U" hand downward on the chin, with added expression.

Take a few minutes to review the signs before making a meal or setting the table. Then, just before you handle that item, see if you can remember how to sign it.

Making Dinner

It is time for dinner. Perhaps this evening you will stay in and cook. You'll go into the kitchen, look inside the refrigerator, and see what there is to eat. It appears the selections for dinner are meat, baked potato, and fish. Then again, it would be simple to just boil some spaghetti, and serve it with bread and butter. In the meantime, while dinner is cooking, you'll set the table.

To sign "dinner" or "supper," form the signs "night" and "eat." Together they create the sign. Variations: To sign "dinner," gently tap your mouth using the "D" hand. To sign "supper," gently tap your mouth using the "S" hand. These versions are initialized signs.

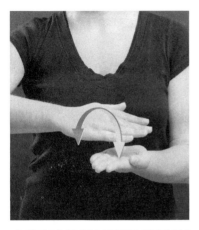

COOK: To sign "cook," flip the "flat" hand back and forth on the palm of your stationary left hand.

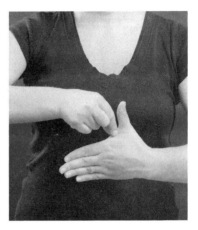

MEAT: Use your index finger and thumb to pinch the meaty part of your left hand between your thumb and index finger.

To sign "kitchen," flip the "K" hand back and forth on the palm of your stationary left hand. This version is an initialized sign.

OVEN, BAKE: Slide the "flat" hand, palm up, under the left "flat" hand, imitating sliding a pan into an oven.

POTATOES: Tap the curved "V" hand on the back of your left fist, imitating piercing a baked potato.

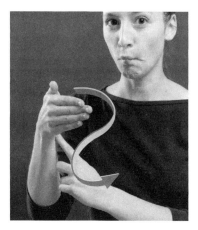

FISH: Move your extended arm, palm facing left, forward in a wiggling motion, imitating a swimming fish.

BOIL: Wiggle the fingers of your right "curved five" hand under your left palm, imitating the heat under the pan bringing it to a boil.

Spaghetti is a fun sign to form, and one that people always seem to remember. The sign imitates how pasta looks when it comes out of a pasta maker. However, you can't eat the pasta until you boil the water.

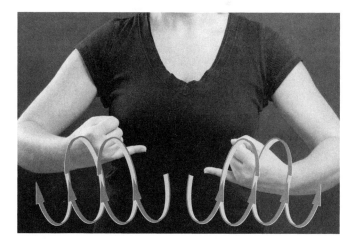

SPAGHETTI: Touch the fingertips of both "I" hands together and pull them apart while forming a circular, curly motion.

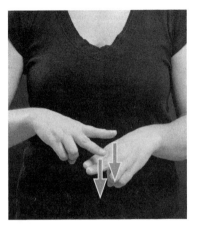

BREAD: Move the edge of your "flat" hand up and down on the back of your left hand, imitating slicing bread.

SALT: Tap your extended index and middle fingers of your right hand on the extended index and middle fingers of your left hand.

To sign "pepper," imitate holding a peppershaker and shake gently.

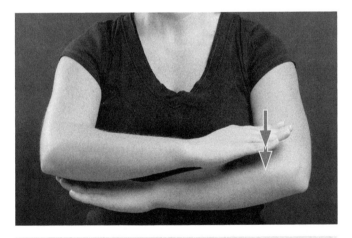

TABLE: Place both arms across the front of your body, right on top of left, palms facing down, and tap your right palm to your left elbow, imitating a tabletop.

The "table" shown in this image is the one that is used to imply that things are set up on the "table," such as plates and cups.

Keep in mind that another sign for "table" is included later in this chapter, which demonstrates the simple structure of a table. Don't get confused. The image above is the correct image to use when you are talking about "food on the table."

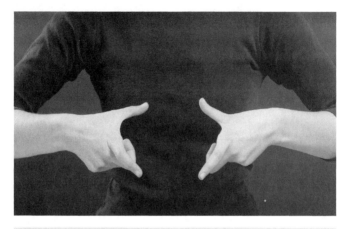

PLATE: Hold both bent "L" hands together.

To sign "bowl," use both "C" hands. The size of the plate or bowl is indicated by how close or far apart the hands are held.

Next, you will need to draw on your memory. These types of applications are a good way to dust off the cobwebs and apply your new knowledge. The next few signs are mimed or use the handshapes of signs that have previously been shown.

- Napkin: Use your "flat" hand and mime dabbing or wiping your mouth with a napkin.
- Spoon: Scoop your right "H" hand, curved like a spoon, into your curved left palm. This sign is formed the same as "soup," but you do not bring it toward your mouth.
- Fork: Jab the inverted "V" into your "flat" left hand.
- Cup/Glass: Use the handshape of "C."
- Water: Tap the "W" hand on the lips, chin, or corner of your mouth.
- Wine: Circle the "W" hand near the corner of your mouth in a backward motion.
- Beer: Move the "B" hand in a backward motion twice near the corner of your mouth.

Dessert, Finally!

The selections from this dessert menu are cake, pie, and ice cream.

DESSERT: Touch the fingertips of your "D" hands several times.

CAKE: Pull the "C" hand across your left "open" palm, imitating pulling out a slice of cake.

PIE: Use your "flat" hand to slice an imaginary piece of pie in your left "open" palm.

CHOCOLATE: Circle the "C" hand on the back of your left hand.

To sign "vanilla" circle the "V" hand on the back of the left hand.

The sign for ice cream is fully mimed. As a child, there is a good chance that you mimed this sign before you attained your verbal skills. All you need to do is hold the cone and lick your imaginary ice cream.

Imagine it is the end of the day and you are planning to unwind. Pop some popcorn, and pour yourself a drink before you settle in front of the television for a while. To sign "TV," fingerspell the letters "T" and "V." This makes the "loan" sign for "television/TV." To sign "thirsty," stroke your index finger down the outside of your throat. To form the sign for a drink of Seven-Up, first sign the number "7," then with your index finger, point upward. Form this combination of these two signs as smoothly as possible. Learning to combine and execute two or more signs smoothly gets you well underway to becoming a good signer.

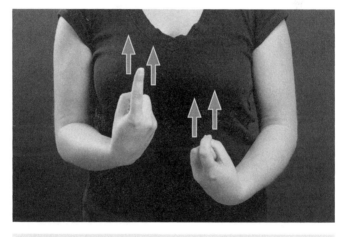

POPCORN: Flick both index fingers alternately, imitating popping corn. *Memory aid*: The flicking fingers imitates how popcorn appears when it is "popping."

Learning all these food items has probably made you hungry. Do you remember how to sign "hungry"? If you answered yes, good for you; it was the first sign in this chapter!

Keep up the good work!

Vocabulary for Home

American Sign Language is really all about describing. When it comes to describing things around the house, there is one particular handshape that is used repeatedly—the "flat" hand. You were introduced to the "flat" hand, with the thumb neatly tucked at the side of the hand (also known as the modified "B"), in Chapter 1. The use of this handshape provides the signer with accuracy for describing things that are flat. Using the "flat" hand will empower you as a signer. As you acquire the following vocabulary for things around the house, you will see the power of the "flat" hand again and again.

HOME: Tap and move the fingertips of the modified "O" hand from the corner of your mouth to the soft part of your cheek. *Variation:* The first variation is to tap the fingertips of the modified "O" hand twice on the soft part of your cheek. The second variation is to tap the fingertips of the flattened "O" hand near the corner of your mouth, then open to a "flat" palm against the cheek.

All of these signs represent "home" as the place where you would eat and sleep. Perhaps you are staying in a college dorm. There is an initialized sign for this word. To sign "dorm," tap and move the "D" hand from the corner of your mouth to the soft part of the cheek.

In Chapter 2, you learned how to sign "house" by making the shape of a roof with both "flat" hands. In Chapter 3, you learned how to make a "room," again using just both "flat" hands. Remember, to sign "room," use both "flat" hands and move them in a box shape to indicate two sets of walls; front and back, and both sides. This sign is also used for "box."

It is important to put to memory the sign for "room." This sign is used as an add-on when describing additional rooms around the house.

BEDROOM: Place both hands, palm to palm, on the side of the face, imitating sleep, and add the sign for "room."

- To sign "living room," combine "live" (see Chapter 2) and "room."
- To sign "dining room," combine "food/eat" (illustrated earlier in this chapter) and "room."

Each chapter introduces vocabulary and gives you an opportunity to build sentences and learn compound signs, as evident in these last two signs.

Take a quick look back at Chapter 3 and practice the following words:

- FLOOR: Use the "flat" hands, palms down, thumbs touching, then separate them, imitating a flat surface.
- WALL: Use the "flat" hands, palms out, thumbs touching, then separate them, imitating a wall.
- WINDOW: Use "flat" hands, palms facing your chest, right hand on top of your left hand, raise your right hand, imitating opening a window.

Earlier in this chapter, you learned how to sign "table." The next sign is a variation of "table," and one that will allow you to form different types and shapes of tables. To sign this next version of "table," use the "flat" hands, palms down, thumbs touching, then separate them, imitating a flat surface. To add legs to the table, use the "G" hands moving downward. You can mold and shape any type of table using these basic handshapes.

All of these signs use some form of the "flat" hand classifier. In this chapter, you begin to see the power and the multiple applications of classifiers, as described in Chapter 3.

Computer Signs

Computers have opened the door to the world. Web cameras on computers offer communication opportunities as never seen before for the deaf and hard of hearing. There are free services for the deaf and hard of hearing, enabling anyone to conduct video relay calls with family, friends, or businesses using certified ASL interpreters via a high-speed Internet connection and a video relay. Computers are a way of life today, so you need to learn some basic computer signs. Many of them are very easy and not as technical as you might think.

COMPUTER: Place the "C" hand on the back of your left hand and move up the arm.

To sign "laptop/notebook": Place hands horizontally in front of you palm to palm. Next, fold back your right hand so the palm faces you, imitating opening a laptop. The bottom hand represents the keyboard portion, and the upper hand represents the screen; add the sign "computer."

FILE: Place the "flat" hand, horizontal, palm up, between the index and the middle fingers on your left hand, then between the middle and the ring fingers. *Memory aid*: The open fingers of the left hand are the slots for the files.

PROGRAM: Flip the "P" hand up over the tops of the fingers and down the back of the left vertical "flat" hand.

INTERNET/NETWORK: Touch the fingertips of both middle fingers of your "open five" hands and pivot back and forth. *Memory aid*: This sign demonstrates connectivity with information moving back and forth.

The sign for e-mail has many variations. Each variation has a different visual value and varying popularity.

E-MAIL 1: To sign "e-mail," form the letter "C" with the left hand, pass the right flat hand through the "C" hand. This variation represents the iconic symbol shown on computers that depicts an envelope.

E-MAIL 2: To sign "e-mail," form the letter "C" with the left hand, extend the right index finger, point forward, and pass through the letter "C." When this sign is reversed, it represents contact in receiving mail.

DISK: Circle the "D" hand in a double clockwise circle in your left upturned palm.

Here's another opportunity to combine two signs you have already learned: "computer" and "bug" (Chapter 4) equals a "virus." If you have a virus, you might need a firewall. This sign is a combination of "fire," shown here, and "wall," shown earlier in the chapter.

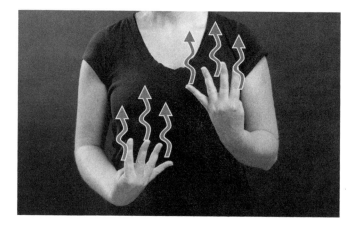

FIRE: Hold both "open five" hands, palms facing in. Wiggle your fingers while moving your hands alternately up and down.

To sign "cursor," move the "X" hand, palm forward, in an upward and forward jagged movement, and visualize the "cursor" moving all around the computer screen.

To sign "window" in relationship to computers, sign it the same way it was demonstrated earlier.

Abbreviations are used throughout the language of computers. Here's another chance to practice, improve, and build your fingerspelling skills.

Word	Abbreviation
Computer disk	CD
Digital Video Disk	DVD
Central Processing Unit/Processor	CPU
Instant Messaging	IM
Software	SW
Gigabyte	GB
Megabyte	MB
Web	WEB
World Wide Web	WWW
Uniform Resource Locator	URL

This preceding group of signs has taught you something new and useful while providing you with the opportunity to review your fingerspelling skills. A good way to remember signs is to teach them to someone else. Perhaps you can share some of these signs with family or coworkers. Remember, to teach is to relearn.

In the Classroom and at the Office

Think back to your early years in elementary school. Visualize your teacher standing in front of the class, clapping her hands, and saying, "Come on, children, it's time to settle down and put our thinking caps on!" Making visual associations, such as this one, adds clarity to the formation of some signs. Now get ready to play school and learn additional sign vocabulary, including many signs for the adult version of school—work!

To sign "school," clap your hands twice. You have made the sign for school, just like the teacher. In Chapter 2, you learned the sign for "teach." The sign for "education" is formed in the same manner this time using both "E" hands on the sides of your forehead and pushing forward slightly. This is another initialized sign.

There is a special way to demonstrate the school years, freshman through senior. Tap the right index finger on the appropriate finger of the left "open five" hand, like so:

- Freshman: tap the ring finger.
- Sophomore: tap the middle finger.
- Junior: tap the index finger.
- Senior: tap the thumb.

Another variation, using the same fingers, for indicating the school years: tap your right thumb, index, middle finger, or ring finger into the palm of the left hand.

School Subjects

Do you remember your favorite subject in school? Here are four subjects for you to sign.

ENGLISH: Use your right hand to cover the back of the left "flat" hand then pull it toward you.

MATH: Cross the "M" hands repeatedly.

SCIENCE: Use both alternating "A" hands, point thumbs down, and make a pouring motion, imitating measuring liquids from science beakers.

ART: Use the "I" hand and draw a wavy motion down your left palm, imitating drawing.

Working in Education

This vocabulary is beneficial to all students of sign language, but it is most important for those who work in educational settings. Sit up straight, pay attention, and let's get down to business. In Chapter 2, the sign for "learn" was demonstrated: you place all the fingertips into your left palm, pull upward with a modified "O" hand, and place it on your forehead, imitating placing knowledge into your mind. If you are a student, you are in school to learn. In order to form the sign for "student," form the sign for "learn" and then add the "person" sign. The sign for "book" is another natural gestural sign. Place both palms together then open, just like a book.

The next signs are all formed in the left palm just as you just signed "art."

- To sign "dictionary" use the "D" hand and stroke your left palm, imitating turning pages in a book.
- To sign "read," use the "V" hand, representing a pair of eyes, move left to right on your left palm, imitating reading.
- To sign "write," mimic writing on your left palm.

■ To sign "graduate," form a clockwise circle with the "G" hand and bring it down into your left palm. Memory aid: The hand movement represents placing a seal on a diploma.

Punctuation

As you know, gesturing and mime are both part of ASL. With that in mind, let's learn how to form punctuation. All of the following punctuation marks are traced in the air exactly as though you were writing them. Remember to make these five punctuation marks large enough so that they can be seen easily by the sign reader.

Punctuation Mark	Symbol
Question mark	?
Exclamation point	!
Quotation marks	" "
Colon	:
Semicolon	;

The sign for "exam," "test," or "quiz" somewhat forms a double-handed question mark. Begin by using both index fingers of the "one" hands; while moving downward, change your index fingers into the shape of the letter "X"; end with both hands in an "open five," palms down.

College Years

You are doing so well at this point that it's time to move on to the college level, to graduate, and to get your diploma.

COLLEGE, UNIVERSITY: Begin with your hands in the same position as "school." Swing your right hand in a counterclockwise upward arc.

Variations for college and university often use "initializations" while maintaining the same movement as described above. Here are a few examples:

- College: Use the right "C" hand
- University: Use the right "U" hand

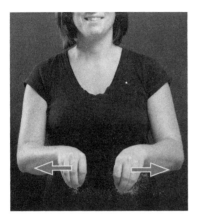

DIPLOMA: Touch the "O" hands together and draw them apart, imitating the shape of a rolled diploma.

As you progress through the material in these chapters, you are made aware of how important it is to know and have command of the handshapes of the alphabet. Another good way to practice fingerspelling is to use this table of abbreviations for specific academic degrees.

Degree	Fingerspelled Abbreviation
Bachelor's of Arts	BA
Bachelor's of Science	BS
Bachelor's of Science in Nursing	BSN
Doctor of Dental Science	DDS
Doctor of Education	EdD
Education Specialist	EdS
Juris Doctor (law degree)	JD
Doctor of Medicine	MD

At Work

Work is described in many different ways because it varies from one person to the other. Whether your job requires going to school full-time, taking care of children, or working as a service provider, it is all described as work. As shown in Chapter 2, to sign "work," use both "S" hands, palms facing down. Tap your right wrist on the back of your left fist a few times. The sign for work can have movement variations that are used to indicate intonation and degree of intensity. When signing "work," you can demonstrate how hard you might have worked by increasing the intensity and the speed with which one hand strikes against the other. Suppose you had a rare day at work when things went smoothly. You can also demonstrate this kind of easy workday by changing the intensity to a slower, softer tapping of the fists.

So it's off to work you go. The start and the end times of your job are very important. You've already learned some of the time signs in Chapter 5; therefore, you know how to point to your watch to indicate time. Now you'll learn how to sign "start" and "stop."

BEGIN, START: Place the index finger of the "one" hand between the index and middle finger of your left hand and turn. *Memory aid*: Visualize placing the key in the ignition of a vehicle and turning it.

Don't limit the sign "start" just to the application of starting a vehicle. Think of this sign when you need to sign: "commence," "origin," "root," "initiate," "activate," "instigate," or "set in motion."

The sign for "start" can be combined with many signs you have learned in previous chapters. With the following exercise, you can expand your vocabulary from singles to pairs. Here's how it works. Start with a basic phrase describing a common action. You visualize this action then sign the words that make it into a series of complete sentences. As you sign the words in the sentences, don't be hesitant to throw in a little mime and gesture. All the words in these three sentences you know how to sign. Visualization is a great tool. Use it, and you will sign successfully. (Quick reminder: you do not need to sign any of the little words people say daily, such as "the," "a," or "is.") Sign the following short sentences:

You wake up in the morning and then you . . .

- Start to make the coffee.
- Start cooking the breakfast.
- Start the car.

The simplest way to sign these sentences:

- Start coffee.
- Start cook breakfast.
- Start car.

If you signed these sentences correctly, congratulations! Sign language is a visual language, and it is how you see the words not how you hear the words. This part of the journey often is the most difficult. Hang in there.

Here are some more work-related signs for you to learn:

STOP: Use the side of your "flat" hand to hit your left "open" palm once.

FINISH: Use "open five" hands, palms facing in, and snap them outward to the sides.

MAKE: Place "S" hands one on top of the other, then twist them back and forth.

HELP: Place the "A" hand in your left "open" palm and lift both hands upward.

In Chapter 1, you learned to sign the initialized version of "boss" by tapping the "B" hand on the heart. Here is another way to sign "boss": tap the "claw" hand on the right shoulder, representing the person who has the responsibility.

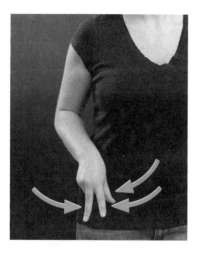

BEEPER/PAGER: Hold the "S" hand at the waist, flick your thumb, index finger, and middle finger, imitating vibration or pulsing.

"Office" is an initialized sign and it is formed with the same movements as "room." To sign "office," use the "O" hands and move them in a box shape to indicate two sets of walls; front and back, and both sides.

Presently, these signs for "fax" are the most popular versions:

- FAX: Move the right "X" hand under the "flat" palm down left hand.
- FAX: Form the letter "F" at the wrist of the left hand, then quickly change to "X" while sliding across the open palm to the end of the fingertips.

In this chapter, you have been all around and about learning common everyday signs. Keep applying the signs you know, especially the signs you just learned, at home or at work daily.

Hitting the Road

Whether you are planning a vacation or you work in travel and tourism, you'll need to learn some vocabulary to get around in new environments (and to describe your adventures when you get back home!). You'll also need to learn about the different versions of signs you might encounter along the way.

Time for a Vacation

Here are five commonly used signs that come in handy when describing a vacation.

VACATION, HOLIDAY: Place the thumbs of the "open five" hands at your armpits then wiggle your fingers.

TICKETS: Grasp the left "flat" hand with the bent "V" hand, imitating punching a ticket.

VISIT, TRAVEL: The "V" hands are rotated alternately, imitating people traveling. Rotating the "V" hand-shape away from you indicates that you are traveling. Rotating the "V" handshape toward you indicates people visiting you.

In the event that you are talking about animal travel, all you need to do is make a small change; form a bent "V" and move forward in a zigzag fashion. With one hand, you could demonstrate a bunny hopping; with both hands, you could demonstrate a leopard stalking.

Vacation always means packing, whether it's the car or the luggage. You know how to sign "vacation," now you need to know how to sign "luggage." The magic word is mime-sign. To sign "luggage," imitate lifting the handle of the luggage. However, with the new style of "luggage," you would imitate pulling a piece of luggage that has wheels.

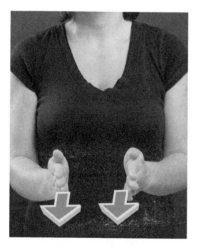

ROAD: Place both "flat" hands palms facing, then move both hands forward.

Many different variations can be applied in the sign for "road." If the road is narrow or wide, bring your hands closer or farther apart. When the road or path is a winding way, simply demonstrate this by moving your hands in a wavy fashion. By using your "R" or "W" hands in the same fashion, the sign for road can be initialized. Knowing this little piece of information might save someone from becoming lost trying to find a street, way, avenue, or road. You have the ability to demonstrate the difference along with the newfound ability to give directions.

Here is a fun sign that closes your journey around the world. Bon Voyage!

HELICOPTER: With your left hand, form the three-finger classifier. Place your right "open five" hand on the tip of your thumb and shake your right hand demonstrating the movement of the blades of the helicopter.

Sign Variations

Often, people wonder if signs are the same all across the United States. The answer is no. There are regional sign variations. These variations can be seen in the formation, placement, or direction of the signs. Nearly all large cities have variations in proper name signs. They also have finger-spelled abbreviations that are specific to the geographical area. For the most part, it is quite easy to adapt to these small and sometimes subtle sign differences. The variations can be compared to the various accents that you hear across the United States.

The variations in signs require signers to be flexible. Staying flexible is one of the important traits that will aid you in your journey to become a terrific signer. Keep in mind that the best signer is not necessarily the one who has the biggest sign vocabulary. The best signer is the one who knows how to *use* the vocabulary he has acquired.

While you are learning sign language, keep in mind the following list of positive traits that will help to make you a well-rounded signer. A good signer will do the following:

- Know more than one way to sign a word
- Be flexible in acquiring signed vocabulary
- Be flexible in applying a variety of signs

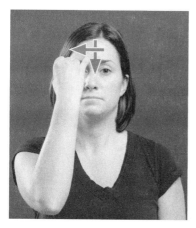

ITALY: Use the "I" hand to draw a cross in the middle of the forehead.

GREECE: Draw the "G" hand down your forehead and nose in a double movement. *Memory aid*: Imitates the profile of Grecian statues.

You have traveled over a small portion of Europe and must include England. Believe it or not, you already know how to sign this country. Earlier in this chapter, you learned how to sign "English." To form the sign for "England" and "Britain" you simply sign "English." Now let's take this sign a bit further, back to the United States, and learn how to form the sign for "New England."

NEW: Move the right "curved" hand, palm up across the palm of your left hand from fingertips to heel, and off the hand in an upward arc.

To sign "New England" simply sign "new" and "England."

Here are two interesting signs: one that imitates the shape of the country, and one that imitates the style of the country's traditional clothing.

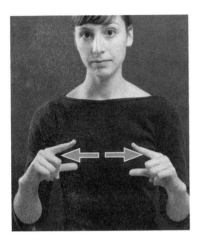

JAPAN: Touch the fingertips of both "G" hands together, then pull them apart to the side of your body, pressing your thumb tips and index tips together. *Memory aid*: Imitates the shape of the Japanese islands.

Abroad, one might see this sign being formed by imitating the sheath covering on a Samurai sword being pulled downward.

CHINA: Point with your index finger to your left shoulder, cross to your right shoulder, and then draw the index finger straight down. *Memory aid*: This sign follows the lines of Chinese traditional clothing.

As a novice signer, you should be mindful when browsing ASL dictionaries—older signs can be disparaging. Cultural awareness and sensitivity is found in the newer versions of how signs are formed. Sign

Appendix A / Quizzes and Games

Alphabet Quiz

Fill in the blanks with the appropriate letter from the Manual Alphabet.

1. To form the letter _____, cross the index and middle fingers. Thumb, ring, and pinky fingers are tucked into the palm.

2. To form the letter _____, all fingers are vertical with the thumb to the palm.

3. To form the letter _____, make a fist, hold the pinky finger vertical.

4. To form the letter _____, place the thumb between the index and middle fingers. Ring and pinky fingers are tucked into the palm. Drop your wrist downward.

5. To form the letter _____, make a fist. Tuck the thumb between the index and middle fingers.

6. To form the letter _____, extend the thumb and pinky finger. Tuck index, middle, and ring fingers into the palm.

7. To form the letter _____, place all fingers on the thumb except for the index finger, which remains vertical.

8. To form the letter _____, place the thumb between the index and middle fingers, hold vertically. Ring and pinky fingers are tucked into the palm.

9. To form the letter _____, pinch the index finger to the thumb. Middle, ring, and pinky fingers are vertical.

10. To form the letter _____, place your index finger on top of your middle finger facing left, with the thumb tucked away behind the two fingers.

Sign Practice Quiz

Read each question and fill in the blank with the appropriate word.

1. To sign "_____" place your palm on your chest.

2. To sign "_____" cross and tap the "H" hands twice.

3. To sign "_____" clap hands twice.

4. To sign "_____" stroke the "curved" hand twice on the left "flat" palm.

5. To sign "_____" raise both hands high in the air in an "open five" position and shake them.

6. To sign "_____" draw the "T" hand down the cheek.

7. To sign "_____" squeeze one or both "S" hands alternately up and down.

8. To sign "_____" place the fingertips of the "open" palms on the chin, then bring down the palms facing up.

9. To sign "_____" place all the fingertips into the left palm. Next, pull upward with a modified "O" hand and place it on the forehead.

10. To sign "_____" place the "flat" hand to the chin, then bring the hand down, palm up, and place it in the left palm.

11. To sign "_____" use the "flat" hand, move it forward and down.

12. To sign "_____" place both "flat" hands palms facing, move both hands forward.

13. To sign "_____" use the "open five" hand, starting at the chin, move clockwise in front of the face, and end with a closed fist.

14. To sign "_____" use the "flat" hand, palm facing back, and push it over the shoulder.

15. To sign "_____" touch the tips of both "I" hands and pull them apart in a circular motion.

16. To sign "_____" place the index and middle fingertips into the left "open" palm.

17. To sign "_____" circle the "flat" hand on the chest clockwise.

18. To sign "_____" place the fingertips of both hands on the chest and rock back and forth.

19. To sign "_____" use both "flat" hands, palms facing each other, and move hands straight down.

20. To sign "_____" place the "flat" hand at the temple.

21. To sign "_____" place the "S" hand at the temple and then snap open the index finger.

22. To sign "_____" move the "F" hands from each side of the mouth outward.

23. To sign "_____" twist "F" hands alternately back and forth several times, then add "person."

24. To sign "_____" rub the right "H" hand back and forth on top of the left "H" hand.

25. To sign "_____" use the "S" hands, closed fists facing up, and open hands quickly many times.

Quiz Answers

Alphabet Quiz Answers

1.	R	**5.**	T	**8.**	K
2.	B	**6.**	Y	**9.**	F
3.	I	**7.**	D	**10.**	H
4.	P				

True/False Awareness Quiz Answers

Questions 1 through 9 are all True. Question 10 is False—there are twenty-six letters in the English alphabet. Just checking to see if you were snoozing!

Letter Form Quiz Answers

1. A E M N O S T are formed with a closed hand.
2. B C D F I K L R U V W X Y are formed in a vertical position.
3. G H are formed in a horizontal position.
4. P Q are formed pointing downward.

Sign Practice Quiz Answers

1.	My, mine	**8.**	Thank you	**15.**	Spaghetti	**22.**	Cat
2.	Name	**9.**	Learn	**16.**	Stand	**23.**	Interpreter
3.	School	**10.**	Good	**17.**	Please	**24.**	Train
4.	Excuse	**11.**	Future	**18.**	Animal	**25.**	Many
5.	Applause	**12.**	Road	**19.**	Person		
6.	Tan	**13.**	Beautiful	**20.**	Know		
7.	Milk	**14.**	Past	**21.**	Understand		

Sign Language Games

ABC Game

Starting with the first letter of the alphabet, each person will finger-spell an item in the selected category. Each person will repeat all previous fingerspelled words before adding her own selection. No duplicating is allowed. The categories can be of your choosing—for example: food, clothing, animals, occupations, furniture, drinks, plants, books, movies, music/musical instruments, etc. The last person can choose the next category. This game can also be played with signs instead of fingerspelling each word or both signs and fingerspelling can be combined during the game.

Color Game

Sign or fingerspell as many items as you can in thirty seconds that are the color red, blue, green, yellow, orange, white, pink, purple, brown, or black. This game requires a larger acquisition of signs.

Facial Expression and Body Language Game

A narrator reads a children's story, such as "Goldilocks," "The Three Little Pigs," "Snow White," or "Cinderella." Friends, family members, or students act out the parts using facial expression, body language, mime, and gestures. Only limited sign is needed for this game.

Knock Knock Game

There is a knock on the door. The player opens an imaginary door, and using facial expression, body language, mime, and gesture only, she will attempt to convey the message on the index card. Write any of the following, plus whatever else you may want to invent, on an index card for each player.

Knock Knock, open the imaginary door:

- You find a very large box wrapped up in beautiful paper, but it is too big to bring it through the door.
- You find a puppy.
- You find a man delivering a vase with roses.
- You find something very disgusting and slimy.

- You find a bag of rubbish.
- You find one million dollars.
- You find a very heavy box.
- You find a family of raccoons.
- You find another door.
- You find an old friend.
- You find a pizza delivery.
- You find a full-length mirror.
- You find a tornado.
- You find a photographer snapping your picture.
- You find a shiny new _____.

Brown Bag Game

Place three to five items in a small brown paper bag. Then describe each item using signs, fingerspelling if needed for brand names, acting out using the item if applicable, facial expression, body language, mime, and gestures. A more advanced level of this game can be played by placing three to five items in a brown bag that have related importance to the player. The player will describe each item and why the item is important to her. Examples:

- A bag of beach sand from a fabulous vacation getaway
- A picture of a family member, a pet, place, or thing
- A souvenir from high school, college, and so on
- A letter, a book, or a movie ticket
- Collectables, a piece of jewelry, and so on

Sign Opposites Game

One person signs a sentence or a single sign and the other person signs the opposite. Examples:

- Up / Down
- Winter / Summer
- Start the car / Stop the car
- Open the door / Close the door

Household Game

A person will act out the function of a household object. The receivers give the sign or write out the name of the object. Examples:

- Unlocking a door: a key
- Washing dishes: dish liquid or a dishwasher
- Cleaning the floor: a broom, vacuum, or mop

Twins Game

Choose a category such as trees, food, clothing, animals, or colors. Players are set up in pairs. A signal to start is given, and both players simultaneously fingerspell or sign only one item from the selected category. If the players fingerspell or sign the same item, they receive a point. The team with the most points wins.

Appendix B / Resources

Deaf/Sign Language Resources

ADCO Hearing Products, Inc.
5661 South Curtice Street
Littleton, CO 80120
Voice/TTY: 303-794-3928 or 800-726-0851
www.adcohearing.com

ALDA, Inc.
1131 Lake Street #204
Oak Park, IL 60301
Voice/Fax: 877-907-1738
TTY: 708-358-0135
www.alda.org

Americans with Disabilities Act
United States Department of Justice
Civil Rights Division
Voice: 800-514-0301
TTY: 800-514-0383
www.usdoj.gov/crt/ada

AT&T Relay Center
Relay Center Access: 800-855-2881
800-682-8786
www.consumer.att.com/relay/tty/index.html

Clarion by Advanced Bionics
Corporate Headquarters
Advanced Bionics Corporation
12740 San Fernando Road
Sylmar, CA 91342
Voice: 661-362-1400 or 800-678-2575
TTY: 800-678-3575
www.cochlearimplant.com

CODA International, Inc.
P.O. Box 30715
Santa Barbara, CA 93130-0715
www.coda-international.org

Dawn Sign Press
6130 Nancy Ridge Drive
San Diego, CA 92121-3223
Voice/TTY: 858-625-0600
www.dawnsign.com

Deafness Research Foundation
Hearing Health Magazine
641 Lexington Avenue, 15th Floor
New York, NY 10022
Phone: 212-328-9480
Fax: 212-328-9484
www.drf.org

Families for Hands and Voices

P.O. Box 371926
Denver, CO 80237
303-300-9763 or 866-422-0422
www.handsandvoices.org

Gallaudet University

800 Florida Avenue NE
Washington, D.C. 20002
Voice/TTY: 202-651-5000
www.gallaudet.edu

Garlic Press

1312 Jeppesen Avenue
Eugene, OR 97401
541-345-0063
www.garlicpress.com

Harris Communications

15155 Technology Drive
Eden Prairie, MN 55344-2277
Voice: 800-825-6758
TTY: 800-825-9187
www.harriscomm.com

Hearing Loss Association of America (formerly Self-Help for Hard of Hearing People SHHH)

7910 Woodmont Avenue, Suite 1200
Bethesda, MD 20814
Voice: 301-657-2248
TTY: 301-657-2249
www.hearingloss.org

National Association of the Deaf

814 Thayer Avenue
Silver Spring, MD 20910-4500
Voice: 301-587-1788
TTY: 301-587-1789
www.nad.org

National Education for Assistance Dogs Services (NEADS) National Campus

305 Redemption Rock Trail South
Princeton, MA 01541
Voice/TDD: 978-422-9064
www.neads.org

National Technical Institute for the Deaf

Lyndon Baines Johnson Building
52 Lomb Memorial Drive
Rochester, NY 14623-5604
Voice/TTY: 716-475-6700
www.rit.edu/NTID

National Theatre of the Deaf

139 North Main Street
W. Hartford, CT 06107
Voice: (860) 236-4193 or 800-300-5179
Relay: 866-327-8877
Video: 800-NTD-1967
www.ntd.org

Registry of Interpreters for the Deaf, Inc.

333 Commerce Street
Alexandria, VA 22314
Voice: 703-838-0030
TTY: 703-838-0459
www.rid.org

Sign Media, Inc.

4020 Blackburn Lane
Burtonsville, MD 20866-1167
Phone: 800-475-4756 or 301-421-0268
www.signmedia.com

Soundbytes

108 Industrial Drive
Jersey City, NJ 07305
Voice/TTY: 888-816-8191
www.soundbytes.com

Ultratec
450 Science Drive
Madison, WI 53711
Voice/TTY: 608-238-5400
www.ultratec.com

Websites

ASL Info
www.aslinfo.com/deafculture.cfm

ASL Pro
www.aslpro.com

American Sign Language Fonts
*http://babel.uoregon.edu/yamada/fonts/
asl.html*

American Society for Deaf Children
www.deafchildren.org

ASL Dictionary
www.bconnex.net/~randys

Baby Sign Language
www.babysignlanguage.net
www.babies-and-sign-language.com
www.mybabycantalk.com
www.signingbaby.com

Clerc Center
www.clerccenter.gallaudet.edu

Deaf Education
www.deafed.net

Deaf Life
www.DeafTrivia.com
www.deaf.com

Deaf Missions Official Online/Animated
Dictionary of Religious Signs
www.deafmissions.com

Deaf Net
www.deaf.net

Deaf Performing Arts Network
www.d-pan.com

DeafWeb Washington
www.deafweb.org/natlorgs.htm

Ear Surgery Information Center
www.earsurgery.org

Food and Drug Administration
www.fda.gov

Handspeak
www.handspeak.com

Hearing Health
www.hearinghealth.net

KODA
www.koda-info.org

Life Print
www.lifeprint.com

Michigan State University
*http://commtechlab.msu.edu/sites/aslweb/
browser.htm*

National Association of the Deaf Information Center
www.nad.org/infocenter

Say What Club
www.saywhatclub.com

Signing Online
www.signingonline.com

Sorenson Communications
www.sorenson.com

Sign Language Books

A Basic Course in American Sign Language, by Carol Padden, Tom Humphries, and Terrence O'Rourke.

American Sign Language, "The Green Books," by Charlotte Baker-Shenk and Dennis Cokely.

American Sign Language: A Comprehensive Dictionary, by Martin L. A. Sternberg, EdD.

American Sign Language Medical Dictionary, by Elaine Costello.

American Sign Language Phrase Book, by Lou Fant.

American Sign Language the Easy Way, by David A. Stewart.

Conversational Sign Language II, by Willard Madsen.

Gallaudet Survival Guide to Signing, by Leonard G. Lane.

Handmade Alphabet, by Laura Rankin.

Learn American Sign Language, by Arlene Rice (flashcards and booklet).

Learning American Sign Language, by Tom Humphries and Carol Padden.

Medical Sign Language, by W. Joseph Garcia and Charles C. Thomas.

Random House Webster's American Sign Language Dictionary, by Elaine Costello, PhD.

Religious Signing, by Elaine Costello.

Signing Made Easy, by Rod R. Butterworth and Mickey Flodin.

Signs Across America, by Edgar H. Shroyer and Susan P. Shroyer.

Signs of the Times, by Edgar H. Shroyer.

Talking with Your Hands and Listening with Your Eyes, by Gabriel Grayson.

The Joy of Signing, by Lottie L. Riekehof.

The Joy of Signing Puzzle Book, by Linda Lascelle Hillebrand.

The Joy of Signing Puzzle Book 2, by Linda Lascelle Hillebrand with Lottie L. Riekehof.

The Perigee Visual Dictionary of Signing, by Rod R. Butterworth.

Cochlear Implant Information Resources

Children with Cochlear Implants in Educational Settings, by Mary Ellen Nevins and Patricia M. Chute.

Cochlear Implants: A Handbook, by Bonnie Poitras Tucker.

Cochlear Implants in Children, by John B. Christiansen and Irene W. Leigh.

Hear Again Back to Life, by Arlene Romoff.

The Handbook of Cochlear Implants and Children, by Nancy Tye-Murray.

The Handbook of Pediatric Audiology, by Sanford E. Gerber.

The Parent's Guide to Cochlear Implants, by Patricia M. Chute and Mary Ellen Nevins.

Deaf Literature

A Deaf Adult Speaks Out, Third Edition, by Leo M. Jacobs.

A Loss for Words, by Lou Ann Walker.

A Man Without Words, by Susan Schaller.

American Deaf Culture: An Anthology, by Sherman Wilcox, ed.

Angels and Outcasts: An Anthology of Deaf Characters in Literature, by Trent Batson and Eugene Bergman, eds.

At Home Among Strangers, by Jerome D. Schein.

Deaf History Unveiled, by John V. VanCleve, ed.

Deaf in America: Voices from a Culture, by Carol Padden and Tom Humphries.

Deaf Like Me, by Thomas S. Spradley and James P. Spradley.

Deaf President Now! The 1988 Revolution at Gallaudet University, by John B. Christiansen and Sharon N. Barnartt.

Everyone Here Spoke Sign Language: Hereditary Deafness on Martha's Vineyard, by Nora Ellen Groce.

I Have a Sister—My Sister Is Deaf, by Jeanne Whitehouse Peterson.

Mother Father Deaf: Living Between Sound and Silence, by Paul Michael Preston.

Seeing Voices, by Oliver Sacks.

The Mask of Benevolence: Disabling the Deaf Community, by Harlan Lane.

The Week the World Heard Gallaudet, by J. Gannon.

Train Go Sorry, by Leah Hager Cohen.

What's That Pig Outdoors? A Memoir of Deafness, by Henry Kisor.

When the Mind Hears: A History of the Deaf, by Harlan Lane.

You and Your Deaf Child, by John W. Adams.

Videos and CDs

These titles are easily available online, through any of the resources listed here, or in any of your favorite local bookstores or retailers where videos and multimedia entertainment materials are sold.

The American Sign Language Dictionary (CD-ROM)

American Sign Language Vocabulary (CD-ROM)

Baby See 'n Sign

Children of a Lesser God

Cochlear Implants: Covering the Basics

DEAFology 101: Deaf Culture as Seen Through the Eyes of a Deaf Humorist

From Mime to Sign

Sign with Your Baby

Signing Naturally

Sound and Fury

Appendix C / Glossary

acronym
A word formed from the first letters of several words.

active hand
The dominant hand; that is, the hand that moves when forming a sign.

ADA
Americans with Disabilities Act.

American Manual Alphabet
Twenty-six handshapes that represent the letters of the alphabet.

American Sign Language
A visual language that is the primary means of communication for the Deaf.

audiogram
A graph on which a hearing test result is recorded.

body shift
The movement of the signer's upper torso to represent two or more characters in a story or conversation.

The "Broken Ear"
The National symbol that represents deafness.

classifiers
A set of handshapes that represent categories, shapes, sizes, and movements of objects.

cochlear implant
A device surgically implanted into the skull to stimulate the auditory fibers, allowing certain amounts of hearing.

CODA
Acronym meaning "Children of Deaf Adults."

compound sign
Combining two or more signs.

Contact Sign
A form of communication that uses sign language in English word order and combines both elements of ASL and English. Also referred to as PSE (Pidgin Sign English).

cued speech
A set of eight handshapes used in four different locations around the face and mouth to help a lip reader distinguish between different sounds that look similar.

deaf
The term used to describe the condition in which the sense of hearing is nonfunctional for the purpose of everyday communication.

Deaf community
Deaf people who share common values, experiences, and a language.

decibel
A decibel, or dB, is a unit of measurement for the loudness of sound.

dominant hand
The strong, active hand that is used when signing.

fingerspelling
The application of the manual alphabet to spell out words in full or abbreviated form.

GA
The abbreviation for "go ahead" when typing on a TTY/TDD.

Gallaudet University
The only liberal arts college exclusively for the Deaf in the United States.

gesture
A body movement used in communicating.

grammar
The principles, structure, and rules of a language.

handshape
The shape of the hand, fingers, and palm when forming a sign.

iconic signs
Signs that resemble objects.

initialized signs
Signs that borrow letters from the manual alphabet.

interpreter
A person who translates spoken language into sign language and/or sign language into spoken language.

KODA
Acronym meaning "Kids of Deaf Adults."

lip reading
The ability to observe lip movement in order to understand oral language.

modified signs
Signs that have been changed, compressed, or altered.

nonmanual
Refers to signs that use head movement, facial expression, body language, and eye movement, and do not involve the hands.

OIC
The abbreviation for "Oh, I see" when typing on a TTY/TDD.

oralism
A method of communicating and educating a deaf person without the use of sign language.

postlingual deaf
Term used to describe a person whose deafness occurs after language is acquired.

prelingual deaf
Term used to describe a person whose deafness occurs at birth or before language is acquired.

PSE
Pidgin Sign English, a form of communication that uses sign language in English word order and combines both elements of ASL and English. Also referred to as Contact Sign.

Q
The abbreviation that is used when asking a question during a TTY/TDD conversation.

relay service
A service that provides a connection between a TTY user and a hearing person and uses a communication assistant, referred to as a CA.

sightline
The center of the signer's chest.

sign language
A manual language that uses symbols to represent ideas and concepts.

Signed English
A signing system that is used to represent spoken English.

signer
A person who uses sign language.

"Signer's Hands"
The national symbol representing Interpreters of Sign Language.

signing space
The signing space, which includes the sightline, is the area where the majority of the signs are formed.

sim-com/simultaneous communication
Manual and oral communication used simultaneously.

SK
The abbreviation for "stop keying" when typing on a TTY/TDD.

speech reading
The ability to observe lip movement in order to understand oral language.

synonym
A word that is different from but expresses the same meaning as another word.

syntax
The order in which words or signs are placed to form sentences and phrases.

timeline
An imaginary line through the body extending in front and behind.

total communication
The application of all methods of communicating.

TTY/TDD
A telecommunication device for the deaf that acts as a telephone.

variation
Differences in the formation and production of vocabulary.

Index